"It's so simple: Love God with all your heart, soul, mind and strength, and love your neighbor as yourself. And yet the church today still struggles with 'But who is my neighbor?' Brenda Salter McNeil goes right to the heart of the problem of our faltering witness: We lack the urgency to bring down the barriers that divide us *in* the church, and we don't know how to *live* the gospel in a multicultural society. The chapters on intentionality and needing one another are themselves worth their weight in gold. If only we will listen!"

NETA JACKSON, AUTHOR OF THE YADA YADA PRAYER GROUP NOVELS

"Through real-life stories and practical insights, Brenda Salter McNeil draws our attention to dynamics and values we often fail to address in our comfortable, lowest-common-denominator, minimalist efforts at evangelism. Dr. Salter McNeil gives us the vocabulary of justice, partnership, reciprocity and authenticity that, if heeded, gives us an opportunity for a genuine, authentic and credible witness to an increasingly diverse and rapidly changing cultural context."

SOONG-CHAN RAH, MILTON B. ENGEBRETSON ASSISTANT PROFESSOR OF CHURCH GROWTH AND EVANGELISM, NORTH PARK THEOLOGICAL SEMINARY

"Brenda Salter McNeil has done some wonderful critical thinking about evangelism and how the gospel is to be presented with justice and in a holistic manner. She details how community, race and culture need to be considered in our sharing of the good news. This is a must-read for serious-minded people striving to follow Christ in a postmodern world."

WAYNE "COACH" GORDON, LAWNDALE COMMUNITY CHURCH

"Drawing from Jesus' encounter with the Samaritan woman at the well, Dr. Salter McNeil engages the text in a fresh, insightful and relevant manner that urges the reader to move beyond the limitations of individual evangelism and embrace the much-needed reality of holistic reconciliation. Weaving aspects of her personal journey with the Samaritan woman's story, Dr. Salter McNeil exposes and expounds on the often-neglected interpersonal issues of sexism, elitism, ageism, racism and schism in an affable, poignant and yet convicting manner. I highly recommend and encourage everyone to acquire, read and above all live out the challenges and enduring principles graciously presented by Reverend Dr. Brenda Salter McNeil in *A Credible Witness.*"

LUIS A. CARLO, ASSOCIATE DEAN, ALLIANCE THEOLOGICAL SEMINARY

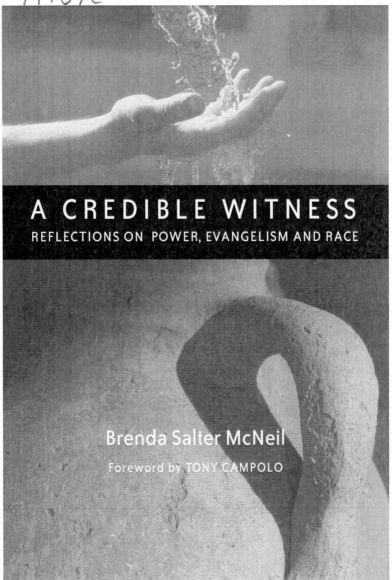

A CREDIBLE WITNESS

REFLECTIONS ON POWER, EVANGELISM AND RACE

Brenda Salter McNeil

Foreword by TONY CAMPOLO

IVP Books

An imprint of InterVarsity Press
Downers Grove, Illinois

InterVarsity Press
P.O. Box 1400, Downers Grove, IL 60515-1426
World Wide Web: www.ivpress.com
E-mail: email@ivpress.com

InterVarsity Press® is the book-publishing division of InterVarsity Christian Fellowship/USA®, a student movement active on campus at hundreds of universities, colleges and schools of nursing in the United States of America, and a member movement of the International Fellowship of Evangelical Students. For information about local and regional activities, write Public Relations Dept., InterVarsity Christian Fellowship/USA, 6400 Schroeder Rd., P.O. Box 7895, Madison, WI 53707-7895, or visit the IVCF website at <www.intervarsity.org>.

Scripture quotations, unless otherwise noted, are from the New Revised Standard Version of the Bible, copyright 1989 by the Division of Christian Education of the National Council of the Churches of Christ in the USA. Used by permission. All rights reserved.

Design: Cindy Kiple
Images: jar: Marje Cannon/iStockphoto
        hand: Heiko Grossmann/iStockphoto

ISBN 978-0-8308-3482-2

Printed in the United States of America ∞

Library of Congress Cataloging-in-Publication Data

McNeil, Brenda Salter, 1955-
  A credible witness: reflections on evangelism, power, and race /
  Brenda Salter McNeil.
    p. cm.
  Includes bibliographical references.
  ISBN-13: 978-0-8308-3482-2 (pbk.: alk. paper)
  1. Samaritan woman (Biblical figure) 2. Witness bearing
  (Christianity) 3. Reconciliation—Religious aspects—Christianity.
  I. Title.
  BS2520.S9M36 2008
  269'.2—dc22

                                                                2007043216

P   18   17   16   15   14   13   12   11   10   9   8   7   6   5

Y   23   22   21   20   19   18   17   16   15   14   13   12

To my children,

Omari Immanuel McNeil and Mia Imani McNeil.

May you come to fully embrace the greatest story ever told.

And to my husband, J. Derek McNeil,

who makes everything I do better.

CONTENTS

FOREWORD

Jesus prayed that we all might be one, but we are anything but "one." There is no way to argue with the statement made by Martin Luther King Jr. that, in America, "11:00 on Sunday morning is the most segregated hour of the week."

There are reasons for the separateness of Christians. Differences in race, social class, economic status, education and cultural identity tend to keep us from interacting with each other. Most of us live out what one sociologist called "consciousness of kind." In simple language, that means we feel comfortable with people whom we find to be like ourselves. The experts in the field of church growth make it clear that the churches that grow the fastest are those which are "homogeneous units." In popular discussions, that comes down to the truism that birds of a feather flock together—and this holds true for Christians as well as for the rest of the population. It holds true in spite of Jesus' prayer that we would all be one.

In the face of this social reality stands the Day of Pentecost. On that day, people from various nations, different socioeconomic backgrounds and diverse ethnic groups came together and, under an outpouring of the Holy Spirit, became one.

Just a little more than a hundred years ago, a historical event occurred in a small clapboard building in Azusa, California, when there was another outpouring of the Holy Spirit on Christians. Again, various kinds of people became one. Harvard scholar Harvey Cox points out in his book *Fire from Heaven* that what characterized this latter movement of the Spirit was not so much the speaking in tongues commonly associated with the Pentecostal movement, but rather the unity of the variety of worshipers at that gathering. Hispanics, blacks, whites, Asians, rich, poor, uneducated and sophisticated—all came together and became one. The Los Angeles newspapers gave extensive coverage to the protracted meetings in that little building. What fascinated the reporters was that people who ordinarily would have had nothing to do with each other were, under the spiritual dynamism of Pentecostal prayer, hugging each other and worshiping God, seemingly without any awareness of the social barriers that hitherto had divided them. It is not surprising that the Pentecostal movement has grown to more than 500 million worldwide. People are thirsty for that which will enable them to sing in perfect harmony.

Today, while more liberal mainline denominational churches pass resolutions that decry racial segregation, they remain, for the most part, decidedly segregated. On the other hand, Pentecostal churches, which are much less inclined to address social issues, tend to have the most diverse congregations in America. Many of us who are not Pentecostal suffer a certain amount of guilt when we observe this. We consider the segregation of our own congregations and want to know what we can do about it.

When it comes to speaking in tongues, it's not that we are opposed to the practice. It's just that it is not part of our regular worship. We seem to be oriented to other ways of experiencing the fullness of the Holy Spirit in our lives. Many of us are taking "spiritual formation" courses and finding that we yearn to embrace long-neglected practices such as those taught by St. Ignatius.

It is because some of us have so much to learn about receiving that charisma of God which our Pentecostal sisters and brothers seem to embrace so effortlessly that this book is necessary. Brenda Salter McNeil explains the steps we can take to help us cross the sociocultural barriers that too often separate Christians and keep us from living out the biblical mandate to "love one another."

Utilizing the scriptural account of the encounter between Jesus and the Samaritan woman at the well, McNeil outlines the ways in which the Lord of history reached across social barriers to establish spiritual connections with a woman who not only hailed from a race the Jews had scorned but who was living a life that made her a moral outcast. McNeil helps us learn from the ultimate teacher how to take the initiative in connecting with those who differ from us. She reintroduces us to the One who "thought it not robbery to be equal with God," emptied himself of power and took on the role of a powerless servant (see Philippians 2:5-10) in his ministry of reconciliation.

Using her own story, Brenda Salter McNeil helps us to understand how an African American woman feels when persons like myself make well-intentioned but fumbling efforts to cross the lines of gender and race out of a sense of obligation stemming from guilt. McNeil does not condemn but instead endeavors to help us understand the feelings and motivations behind our actions, and then to make the right moves toward achieving that unity in Christ which expresses the church at its best.

In the midst of all that she writes, McNeil leaves no doubt that underlying the crosscultural sensitizing that she promotes is the conviction that unless persons are surrendered to Christ as their Lord and Savior, their efforts toward reconciliation within Christendom will not be real.

The Bible refers to the church as God's "showpiece." This means that we are to be a living demonstration in time and space of what God intends for all of humanity in this world, and a foretaste of what heaven will be like. If we Christians are to live up to that calling, we must learn through Scripture and with empowerment from "on high" how to be an answer to Jesus' prayer that we all might be one.

A church that is not unified is a scandal and a contradiction of the gospel. This book is a good place for us to begin in our contemplation of the biblical mandate for us to love one another. Brenda Salter McNeil allows us to look deeply into one African American woman who exemplifies how each of us can be empowered to overcome the social forces of history that have kept us from experiencing the "tie that binds." Her book will guide us on a journey to becoming a countercultural people who truly live out the values of the kingdom of God.

Tony Campolo, Ph.D.

ACKNOWLEDGMENTS

Writing this book has been a labor of love for me. In fact, in many ways it has been a birthing process. I would not have been successful in delivering this book without the love, support and capable assistance of many "midwives" along the way. To each of them I am deeply grateful. I especially want to acknowledge and thank Jo Kadlecek, who was the first person who encouraged me to write. I am also grateful to Patricia Raybon—my favorite author—whose writing inspires me and challenges me to tell the truth. To one of my mentors and role models, Dr. Tony Campolo, thank you for being an example to me of a socially engaged, deeply devoted Christ-follower. I am honored to know you and hope to follow in your footsteps. To my dear friends Ruth Haley Barton, who has been with me throughout this entire writing process, and Dr. Jeanne L. Porter, who helped me to clarify my focus—thank you. To my editors, Cindy Bunch and Ruth Goring, and to the entire staff at InterVarsity Press—you are a Godsend. Thank you for believing in me as a person and as an author. I give special thanks to my business manager, Rob Robinson, who helped me to understand the importance of writing this book, and to Karen Evans, who faithfully prayed for the completion of this project. To Rev. Betzy Cisneros—thank you for your kingdom heart and for the many ways you support me in ministry. I could not have done this without you. To Jimmy McGee, Dr. Kazi Joshua, Stanley E. Stroman, John Swain Jr., D. Wesley Poythress and Dr. Lauren Dungy-Poythress and the IVP readers, I say a heartfelt "thank you" for reviewing the manuscript and giving your feedback. Your insightful comments substantially improved the quality of this work. I am also grateful for Sharisse Jones—a scribe in the biblical tradition—whose contribution greatly enhanced the contents of this book. Thank you to Rosann Swain, Doris Lambert, Father Michael Pfleger and Dr. Robb Thompson for the unselfish way you share your heart, wisdom and life experience so others can see the kingdom of God in action. Also, I thank God for J. Derek, Omari and Mia McNeil. Nothing I accomplish is possible without the love, support and sacrifice of my family. Then last, but not least, I am eternally grateful to Margaret Alma Blackwell Moore and Theodore Alexander Faison, who modeled true Christianity for me and led me into a life-changing relationship with Jesus Christ. I will never be the same. Thank you.

INTRODUCTION

Becoming a Credible Witness

The atmosphere was charged with excitement and I was ready to go! I was preaching at a national conference of Christian leaders about racial reconciliation. The music and testimonies were powerful and compelling. I could hardly wait for my turn to preach. Then suddenly I was conscious of the fact that this was the anniversary of the night that I had become a Christian thirty years earlier at Rutgers University. It had been on this same date.

As I pondered that thought, I had a strong spiritual sense that I was supposed to give an altar call when I began to speak. *An altar call? At a Christian conference?* This didn't make much sense. But I also knew it was not a coincidence that I was preaching on that very night and maybe there *were* people at the conference who were ready to receive Jesus Christ as their Lord and Savior. So when I got up to speak, I took the risk to tell my story, and then I invited anyone who wanted to receive Jesus Christ into their life to raise their hands. To my surprise and gratitude, thirteen people responded and prayed to become Christians. It was exhilarating! That night turned out to be a life-changing experience for me and for many other people.

When I finally started preaching, I spoke from John 4 and explained the principles that I believe are necessary for a person, group or organization to successfully cross cultures and build bridges in a multiethnic world. These principles are based on the paradigm of Jesus' meeting with the woman at the well. Until that night I had never combined them in an evangelistic message with a call to racial reconciliation.

On that anniversary God brought together evangelism and reconciliation for me in a new way. The experience taught me that evangelism and reconciliation are two sides of the same coin. While one side may be more in focus at any given time, the two sides cannot be separated. This link between evangelism and reconciliation is supported by biblical, demographic and global evidence, and seeing the link is necessary for understanding what it means to be a credible witness of the gospel.

THE WHOLE MESSAGE OF THE GOSPEL

On the cross Jesus reconciled us to God, and he also reconciled us to each other—both in the same act of salvation. Because of the death and resurrection of Jesus Christ, there are no divisions or barriers that separate us from God or from each other. To choose Christ is also to choose his community. According to Ephesians 2, Jesus died so that we could have peace with God *and* with each other. As a result of his heroic sacrifice we are now members of God's family—a new, blood-related people group. Men and women, girls and boys, the young and the old, people from different social classes, ethnic backgrounds and religious traditions have been reconciled and are now of the same household.

This is the whole truth of the gospel. It is an unusual and especially compelling truth in a world that is marked by war, broken relationships, racial and ethnic strife, and economic divisions. When people see us living out the reality of being one, multiethnic, multilingual, multicultural and multinational family in Christ, it grabs their attention, piques their curiosity and causes them to wonder what makes us this way. It is what Jesus called us to do in Matthew 5:16 when he said, "Let your light shine before others, so that they may see your good works and give glory to your Father in heaven." A corporate witness to the reality of reconciliation is a perfect demonstration of the gospel. Our unity in the midst of our diversity is one of the most powerful ways we reveal the reality of what Jesus accomplished on the cross.

I saw this demonstrated one summer when a group of college students came to live in an underresourced urban community in Chicago. These students were from different colleges and universities, represented different socioeconomic levels, came from different parts of the country, were from different church traditions, spoke different languages, had different political beliefs, were conservative and liberal, and were Mexican, Black, White, Korean, Jamaican and Chinese. The only thing that united them was their faith in Jesus Christ. For the entire summer they lived together in a large apartment. They lived within walking distance from the community center where they worked as camp counselors and tutors for inner-city children. Every day their neighbors watched as this multiracial, multiethnic, multicultural group of men and women lived together and served their community.

Finally a man in the neighborhood voiced the question that many other people were wondering about: "Why are you all together and what are you doing here?" The corporate witness of these college students had gripped this man without their saying one word to him. As a result they shared their story with him and talked about how they were brothers and sisters in Christ. They explained that their reconciliation was possible because of Jesus. Later that summer that man became a follower of Christ at an outdoor evangelistic rally with many of those students in attendance.

This is what it means to be a credible witness of the gospel. Often when I preach about racial reconciliation, some in the audience assume that I am preaching some kind of liberal, politically motivated "social gospel" that has nothing to do with Jesus Christ! That's unfortunate. It's a shame that Christians have been evangelized without hearing the whole message of the gospel, which says that God is not mad at us, that all barriers that have divided us from God and from each other have been destroyed and that we are now representatives of the kingdom, which is composed of people from every tribe, language and nation.

Evangelism is more than getting people into heaven. It is calling people into a new community, inviting them into the household of God. There has to be a social component to our evangelism. We are not called just to make individual converts. We are called to make disciples who create corporate social change as a part of a new kingdom community that loves the Lord with all their heart, mind, soul and strength and loves their neighbor as themselves (see Luke 10:27). This is the message of evangelism, and it is the message of reconciliation. Evangelism and reconciliation are two sides of the same message. When we don't live like this, proclaiming and calling others to this reality, we produce inept followers of Christ.

REDEFINING EVANGELISM

What does evangelism have to do with social justice and racial and ethnic reconciliation? Everything, if we take Jesus seriously. Jesus models a startling kind of evangelism that loves people deeply, crosses religious, ethnic and sociopolitical barriers, builds relationships of mutuality, and calls us all into profound, far-reaching transformation. This is critical to the future of evangelism, because the world is changing all around us. The demographic evidence demands that we reexamine the methods we use to reach people unlike us.

Worldwide, people are giving their lives to Jesus at an astounding rate. In Africa, the number of people who follow Christ has risen from 3 percent in 1900 to 45 percent today. In China, in the face of sometimes frightening government attacks, an average of about twenty-eight thousand new converts a day are committing themselves to a relationship with Jesus Christ. The vast majority of new Christians are people of color from different countries around the world.

We are not seeing that same rate of Christian growth in the United States. A *Chicago Tribune* article about an atheist summer camp for children cited a 2003 Harris Interactive survey that found that 9 percent of Americans don't believe in God, while another 12 percent are uncertain about God's existence. Christian demographer George Barna, who says, based on his research, that "if you define a Christian as someone who wholly trusts Jesus for their salvation and lives a life of obedience to the commands of God's word then it is true to say that only 10% of Americans are Christians." According to his findings, "9 out of 10 Americans don't know what the Great Commission is, 7 out of 10 haven't a clue what John 3:16 is all about. One third have no idea what the term 'gospel' refers to."*

At the same time, demographic shifts are changing the landscape of the United States, and the implications of these changes for American society and the church are significant. We are becoming an increasingly global and multiethnic nation. The U.S. Census Bureau predicts that the population will more than double by 2100, reaching 571 million. European Americans will represent a smaller percentage of the nation's population. "Census data from March 2002 show that there are 37.4 million Hispanics in the United States and this population is younger with one third of this growing ethnic group under the age of 18 years old." At this rate by 2050, Hispanics will account for 24 percent of people living in the United States. Meanwhile the Asian and Pacific Islander population is projected to grow from about 11.3 million to 37.6 million people. White Americans will make up 53 percent of the United States, compared to 72 percent now.

The number of biracial and multiethnic Americans, not identified with one distinct racial or ethnic group, will continue to grow. A study conducted by veteran demographer Barry Edmonston, summarized in a report titled "The New Americans: Economic, Demographic and Fiscal Effects of Immigration," projects that by 2050 "21 percent of the U.S. population will be of mixed racial or ethnic ancestry, up from an estimated seven percent today." Tiger Woods, the professional golfer, identifies himself as a "Cablinasian"—Caucasian, Black, Native American and Asian. He is an example of this growing shift in the U.S. population. Clearly Christians must become interculturally competent if they are to cross the divides of age, gender, ethnicity, race, class, social status and religion in order to share the gospel.

---

*See notes section for references.

This presents an extreme challenge for many of us because our natural inclination is to approach people who are most like us—people we identify with and feel most comfortable with. Often this means that we speak of our faith only with people whom we can relate to socially, culturally or racially.

When I was younger I used to "witness" to people on my college campus by giving them an evangelistic pamphlet, called a "tract." Usually the tract featured a brief story about someone who experienced a dramatic conversion and was saved from going to hell when they saw the light. I would give these tracts to anyone I encountered. I would also leave them in conspicuous places in hopes that my non-Christian friends and family would find them, read them and give their lives to Christ. This hardly ever happened. Sometimes it would lead to a deeper conversation with someone, but usually they would take the tract and throw it away later. This is "event evangelism," and it often does not take a person's context or culture into consideration. Admittedly almost everyone I "witnessed" to was African American or someone I found easily approachable.

This is an extremely individualistic approach to evangelism that does not call people into a community. We must move beyond this type of event-oriented proclamation evangelism to embrace a more holistic approach, seeing people as *individuals in community.* To do this we must understand whom we are talking to—their culture, their context and the conditions they face.

The message of salvation is more than our verbal proclamation of the gospel. We must redefine evangelism to include how we live and interact with people—what it means for us to call them into God's family to become members of God's household. This is as important as our ability to accurately quote Scriptures.

BEYOND THE "STICK APPROACH"

Jesus modeled this holistic, community-based approach to evangelism for us. More than one type of reconciliation took place between Jesus and the

Samaritan woman in John 4. In that encounter we see a vertical and a horizontal truth intersecting to form the cross. Jesus reconciled the woman back to God, and as a Jewish man he also reconciled with her across religious, ethnic, cultural, social and gender barriers.

In today's world we too are called to embody more than one type of reconciliation. The good news brings us to God, and it also brings life and healing to a broken, dying and divided world. Anything less is not the whole gospel. Far too often well-meaning Christians preach only the vertical truth of the cross: that we have been reconciled to God through Jesus Christ. This is true, but it is only one part of the truth—only one axis of the cross. There is a horizontal reality that must also be declared: that the walls that divided people from one another have been crushed and we are now one blood-related family in Christ. I learned from a dear friend and colleague, Dr. Peter Cha, that to preach anything less is a one-dimensional message that is not the cross but a "stick" that we can use to hit people over the head!

That's what I was doing when I was passing out tracts on my college campus. I had good intentions, but I was trying to convince people to come to Jesus and convert to Christianity by "hitting" them with the fact that they were sinners and needed to be saved so they could experience a new, more fulfilling life. I now know that the "stick approach" to evangelism has caused many people to be hurt by well-meaning Christians like me. Evangelism is more than getting people to change their individual lifestyle or convincing them to convert to Christ. It is about inviting them to join God's family and to join forces with what God is doing in the world. Our evangelism must have a community emphasis in order to be relevant and credible in this increasingly global and multiethnic world.

To reach people with the gospel today we must take seriously the social, structural and global realities that they face. People around the world today are leery of Christianity and often equate it with the materialistic, individualistic and highly sexual images they see portrayed in the media generated by American popular culture. According to a survey by the Pew Global Attitudes Project, people in most Western countries surveyed associate Americans with the positive characteristics "honest," "inventive" and "hardworking." At the same time, substantial numbers also associate Americans with the negative traits "greedy" and "violent." Canadians, who presumably have the greatest contact with Americans, agree with Europeans on the negatives but are less likely to view Americans as honest. And Canada is the only Western nation in which a majority (53 percent) regards Americans as rude. Meanwhile, "Muslim publics, including Indonesians, are highly critical of Americans in many respects. In particular, they are much more likely than others to view the American people as immoral." Although many people from around the world are attracted to the many positive qualities of the United States—its economic prosperity, education, quality health care, civil liberties and political freedoms—they are understandably cynical about the merits of Christianity, which they identify with American culture, and are resistant to being co-opted by it. Furthermore, many cultures outside of North America emphasize the collectivity, the community, and do not place as high a value on individuality as Americans do. They need a Christianity that speaks to their corporate reality and embraces this as a value.

Another global reality is the age gap that is developing between the world's older and younger citizens. "The world's fastest growing age group is comprised of those persons 80 years and older. In 2000, 69 million persons, or 1.1 percent of world population, were aged 80 or older. By 2050, the number aged 80 or older is expected to more than quintuple to 377 million and be 4.2 percent of world population." This is also taking place in the United States; however, it "has an advantage over other developed countries due to its large and growing population of immigrants and minorities. Young families from these groups have much higher fertility rates than the older white population, keeping the U.S. population more youthful."

As the United States continues to undergo rapid growth in its ethnic populations, and as a shift in age distribution results in a widening of the generation gap, it is crucial that we learn to build bridges across racial, age and class divides. Younger Americans seem generally more accepting of cultural diversity and multiethnicity, but they also report feeling "less prepared to engage in relationship building, listening, conflict resolution, and team building, especially across racial and ethnic lines." Although relationships matter to many postmodern young adults and teenagers, they need evidence to believe that national or cultural unity is possible.

TAKING THE WITNESS STAND

The global and national trends I have surveyed will have major implications for evangelism. In this changing milieu our individualistic evangelistic methods are less than effective to reach people who have a collective, relational worldview and tend to be skeptical regarding American Christianity. The future of evangelism will rest on how seriously we take the global postmodern generation and understand the ways that they need us to reach them.

Philosophy professor Bruce Ellis Benson offers a helpful summary of the thinking style that is commonly labeled *postmodern:* "Despite all the differences in postmodern thinkers, they would generally agree that 1) we think and know only in connection with others, 2) our knowledge is always culturally and historically conditioned, and 3) human reason is considerably less powerful than many enlightenment thinkers assumed." In my experience, most postmodern thinkers don't want to be told what to do. They don't believe older adults just because we say something is true. They want to see it in action. They are cynical toward authority figures because they have seen too much duplicity and heard too many expedient promises. This generation is multiracial, global and relational, and we must understand and respect that if we are going to reach them with the gospel. They are more apt to believe that something is true when they have the opportunity to see and experience it for themselves in the context of genuine community.

More than hearing us talk about the gospel, members of the postmodern generation want to see us live it out. If we fail to do this, we will lose credibility as witnesses for the truth of the gospel and the reality of God's kingdom. The loss has already begun. We have only to look at late-night television to see caricatures of Christians as narrow minded and out of touch. Our credibility is in question among people who are searching for answers in a complex, diverse and increasingly hostile world.

The authenticity of the message Jesus came to proclaim about the kingdom of God is on trial. We have been summoned to testify as a witness for the defense. The jury is the world around us, and they will decide, based upon the "preponderance of the evidence," whether Jesus is Lord and his kingdom a reality. Their verdict, in part, will be based upon what they see and hear from us as witnesses.

In conversation with a lawyer friend of mine, I learned that seven factors are necessary to establish a person or a group as a credible witness in a court case:

1. being in the right place
2. being in the right place at the right time
3. being at the right place for the right duration of time
4. seeing the right things
5. being able to relay what was seen with accuracy
6. the life lived prior to this experience
7. not being paid for one's testimony

Credible witnesses can testify only to what they know is true based upon their actual experience. We have to live what we say we believe so we can verify the truth of the gospel on a personal level.

We must be "in the right place at the right time" so we can give a first-hand account of what we know. If we are obedient to God's direction, we will be in the places we are called to be when we are most needed to be there. We will also need to stay there long enough to see and experience the "right things." Our testimony cannot be based solely on what we read in the Bible, hear from other people or are taught in church. It is our *ex-*

perience of the truth and power of the gospel that establishes our credibility. When this is absent, others can attack our integrity because our lives are inconsistent with the kingdom we preach about. But when we "practice what we preach," we can withstand the rigorous scrutiny of any cross-examination, and our life will not discredit us.

As Christians we are on the witness stand for Christ and his kingdom every day. We have been "sworn in," and the jury members have taken their seats. The world around us is deliberating regarding the truth of the gospel. Our testimony must be based upon our actual experience. If we are to regain our credibility as truthful witnesses, we must commit ourselves to living both the vertical and horizontal realities of the cross. This is the type of evangelism that Jesus modeled in his encounter with the Samaritan woman, and it's a strategy that will help us to be more effective in reaching our world.

MY FRIEND SAM

In this book we will take an in-depth exploration of Jesus' encounter with the Samaritan woman. In so doing, we will gain a new understanding of evangelism. We will also take an honest look at ourselves.

The Samaritan woman is often portrayed as an immoral person who was shunned because of her sinful lifestyle, but I believe she has been misunderstood. Indeed, she feels like a familiar friend to me—someone I understand and can relate to. In truth, her story is my story. That's why I've given her a name. I wanted her to be more than a nameless, faceless person in Scripture. I call her Samantha, a gutsy name for a gutsy girl—a survivor. She is my friend Sam, and I'd like to introduce her to you. It's my hope that as you read her story and as I tell mine that you will discover that our stories are not that different from each other's. In fact, you may find that my friend Sam's story is really your story as well. We have a lot in common as people who share the human condition. My friend Sam needed Jesus and so do we. She didn't know it, but that day at the well her life was changed forever because Jesus stepped into her story. He changed what was a tragedy into a romance. He is still doing that today. I know it's true because it happened to me on the last Friday night of October 1974.

So welcome to the well. As we follow the footsteps of Jesus straight to a town in Samaria, we will discover a life-changing approach to sharing the gospel that will revolutionize our evangelism and transcend the cultural, gender, ethnic, socioeconomic and religious boundaries that keep us trapped in tragic stories. Just like my friend Sam, we need a new story—a story that makes sense, a story that's worth living for, a story that tells us who we are and gives us meaning and purpose in life. And then we need to connect our stories together to create a collective narrative that is rooted in the best story of all—that God loves us just the way we are and that our narrative has a plot worth living out because of Jesus Christ.

1

KNOW MY CONTEXT
TO KNOW MY STORY

I first fell in love with John 4 in seminary when Dr. John Perkins led a devotional Bible study on this text. Perkins is cofounder and chair of the Christian Community Development Association, an organization that supports and encourages practitioners of grassroots and church-based efforts to solve problems and meet needs in their own neighborhoods and communities. At that time he and his family were living in Northwest Pasadena, a neighborhood that had one of the highest daytime crime rates in California, where he founded the Harambee Christian Family Center.

As I listened to Perkins's exposition of John 4, I realized that this was the first time I had ever heard someone unpack the social and cultural aspects of this text. Up to then I had heard this Scripture explained only from an evangelistic perspective: the woman in the story was a sinner and public outcast because of her questionable moral character, and Jesus came to the well to save her so she could have eternal life. But as John Perkins taught on this text, I began to see that in order to reach people with the gospel, like Jesus, we must first understand their context.

The story of the Samaritan woman is recorded in John 4:1-42 and is captured beautifully in *The Message*, a contemporary paraphrase of the Bible by Eugene Peterson:

Jesus realized that the Pharisees were keeping count of the baptisms that he and John performed (although his disciples, not Jesus, did the actual baptizing). They had posted the score that Jesus was ahead, turning him and John into rivals in the eyes of the people. So Jesus left the Judean countryside and went back to Galilee.

To get there, he had to pass through Samaria. He came to Sychar, a Samaritan village that bordered the field Jacob had given his son Joseph. Jacob's well was still there. Jesus, worn out by the trip, sat down at the well. It was noon.

A woman, a Samaritan, came to draw water. Jesus said, "Would you give me a drink of water?" (His disciples had gone to the village to buy food for lunch.) The Samaritan woman, taken aback, asked, "How come you, a Jew, are asking me, a Samaritan woman, for a drink?" (Jews in those days wouldn't be caught dead talking to Samaritans.) Jesus answered, "If you knew the generosity of God and who I am, you would be asking me for a drink, and I would give you fresh, living water." The woman said, "Sir, you don't even have a bucket to draw with, and this well is deep. So how are you going to get this 'living water'? Are you a better man than our ancestor Jacob, who dug this well and drank from it, he and his sons and livestock, and passed it down to us?"

Jesus said, "Everyone who drinks this water will get thirsty again and again. Anyone who drinks the water I give will never thirst—not ever. The water I give will be an artesian spring within, gushing fountains of endless life." The woman said, "Sir, give me this water so I won't get thirsty, won't ever have to come back to this well again!" He said, "Go call your husband and then come back." "I have no husband," she said. "That's nicely put: 'I have no husband.' You've had five husbands, and the man you're living with now isn't even your husband. You spoke the truth there, sure enough."

"Oh, so you're a prophet! Well, tell me this: Our ancestors worshipped God on this mountain, but you Jews insist that Jerusalem is the only place for worship, right?" "Believe me, woman, the time is coming when you Samaritans will worship the Father neither on this mountain nor there in Jerusalem. You worship guessing in the dark; Jews worship in the clear light of day. God's way of salvation is made available through the Jews. But the time is coming—it has, in fact, come—when what you're called will not matter and where you go to worship will not matter. It's who you are and the way you live that count before God. Your worship must engage your spirit in the pursuit of truth. That's the kind of people the Father is out looking for: those who are simply and honestly *themselves* before him in their worship. God is sheer being itself—Spirit. Those who worship him must do it out of their very being, their spirits, their true selves, in adoration."

The woman said, "I don't know about that. I do know that the Messiah is coming. When he arrives, we'll get the whole story." "I am he," said Jesus. "You don't have to wait any longer or look any further."

Just then his disciples came back. They were shocked. They couldn't believe he was talking with that kind of woman. No one said what they were all thinking, but their faces showed it. The woman took the hint and left. In her confusion she left her water pot. Back in the village she told the people, "Come see a man who knew all about the things I did, who knows me inside and out. Do you think this could be the Messiah?" And they went out to see for themselves. . . .

Many of the Samaritans from that village committed themselves to him because of the woman's witness: "He knew all about the things I did. He knows me inside out!" They asked him to stay on, so Jesus stayed two days. A lot more people entrusted their lives to him when they heard what he had to say. They said to the woman, "We're no longer taking this on your say-so. We've heard it for ourselves and know it for sure. He's the Savior of the world!"

My friend Sam lived in a context of racial and ethnic strife. The larger society in which she grew up discriminated against her ethnicity, culture, gender and religious tradition. She was a Samaritan woman. Everything in her society suggested, in subtle and not-so-subtle ways, that something was wrong with her—that she was born the wrong ethnicity and the wrong gender. I believe that she knew what it was to be ostracized—to have nothing in the society or popular culture that affirmed her or supported her dignity and worth as a person made in the image of God. So what did it mean to this woman that Jesus was a Jew?

A PAINFUL HISTORY

Samaritans and Jews absolutely did not associate with each other. Their animosity was rooted in their painful shared history after the Assyrians attacked and conquered the northern kingdom of Israel, as recounted in the Old Testament.

The Samaritans are the descendants of two groups: a) the remnant of the native Israelites who were not deported at the fall of the Northern kingdom in 722 B.C.; and b) foreign colonists brought in from Babylonia and Media by the Assyrian conquerors of Samaria (II Kings 17:24ff. gives an account of this). There was theological opposition between these northerners and the Jews of the South because of the Samaritan refusal to worship at Jerusalem. This was aggravated by the fact that after the Babylonian exile the Samaritans had put obstacles in the way of the Jewish restoration of Jerusalem, and that in the 2nd century B.C. the Samaritans had helped the Syrian monarchs in their wars against the Jews. In 128 B.C. the Jewish high priest burned the Samaritan temple on Gerizim.

The Samaritans emerged as a distinct ethnic group whose religious practices were characterized by "unfaithfulness to the covenant established by the God of Israel."

The Samaritans were therefore considered pagans and infidels. Every time Jews encountered Samaritans, they were reminded of the sin, the curse and the disgrace of being defiled by falling into idolatrous pagan practices. Over time the hostility between the Jews and the Samaritans grew to be insurmountable because of their religious and cultural differences. No God-fearing Jew or self-respecting Israelite would be caught dead with a Samaritan. The Jews felt justified in their religious, social and cultural hatred of the Samaritans, who were seen as a debased people—as dogs! To call someone a Samaritan was to hurl an extreme insult.

This type of thinking and name-calling is the beginning of the dehumanization of a person or ethnic group. We objectify and project negative qualities onto those we fear or despise. It is difficult to discriminate against and mistreat a person when you identify with them or think of them as being "like us." However if we can reduce them to "niggers," "terrorists," "savages" or "dogs," or distance them from ourselves as "illegal aliens," they become less than human and acceptable objects of mistreatment. After that, the transition from discrimination to hatred and bigotry becomes easier and easier; racism and "ethnic cleansing" can be justified by well-meaning people as something they are doing to protect the good in the name of the Lord.

A painful example of this is the abuse that happened in Iraq at Abu Ghraib prison. It was reported that while serving as prison guards in the U.S. military, respectable young Americans subjected men and women to violence, severe injury and rape. What could cause normal, patriotic Americans to commit such atrocities? Although there were probably many factors that contributed to this sadistic behavior, "psychologists and historians who study torture give what is probably the most disturbing explanation of all: they are us. For under certain circumstances, almost anyone has the capacity to commit the atrocities seen in the photos that have shocked the world." These guards were normal people in wartime conditions who were afraid and probably saw and referred to the inmates under their care as "the enemy." In this way they objectified and dehumanized them—no longer treating them like people with families who love them, who are innocent until proven guilty, but as objects of war. Most of us would probably like to think that we would never do anything like that. But I have learned firsthand that when someone reduces another person to a category or a derogatory name—something that we all tend to do—they are capable of doing very hurtful things. One day I was at a Christian conference in Wheaton, Illinois, and the keynote speaker was a brilliant scholar who gave one of the most impressive lectures—on gnosticism and its impact on the church and contemporary culture—that I had ever heard. He was outstanding!

At the conclusion of his presentation I decided to ask him a question, but feeling intimidated by his intellectual prowess, I searched for the most intelligent way to articulate my inquiry to prove myself worthy of the time and attention of a man of his stature. I practiced it carefully and formulated the question in my mind before approaching him. The question had to do with racial reconciliation or ethnic diversity; I don't remember the exact phrase I used, but it was one of those two.

However, I do still remember his response. Pointing his finger directly in my face, he yelled at me so everyone around us could hear: "I know your kind!" Then he accused me of being a liberal, left-wing, feminist Democrat who was in favor of gay rights and didn't love our country!

I was hurt and humiliated. His words stung as if he had slapped me in the face. Although I didn't suffer bodily harm, the character assassination was so brutal that I had to be led away by my friends into a nearby stairwell, where I sobbed uncontrollably.

This is what the Samaritans experienced on a daily basis. Like the scholar who felt justified in cutting me down to shreds because he labeled me a "liberal Democrat," assuming he knew my social views and political affiliation, the Jews felt justified in their hatred and mistreatment of the Samaritans. And to be fair, the animosity was mutual: the Samaritans also fueled the bitter hatred between them and the Jews. They did adopt some of the pagan practices and foreign ways of their colonizers, which further validated the Jews in their reasons to stay alienated from them. "The Samaritans received only the five books of Moses, and rejected the writings of the prophets and all the Jewish traditions. From these causes arose an irreconcilable difference between them, so that the Jews regarded them as the worst of the human race and had no dealings with them." To make matters worse, "Samaria became a place of refuge for all the outlaws of Judea. They received willingly all the Jewish criminals and refugees from justice. The violators of the Jewish laws, and those who had been excommunicated, betook themselves for safety to Samaria, and greatly increased their numbers and the hatred which subsisted between the two nations." Hence, there was a long history of mutual hostility between the two ethnic groups, and their hatred for each other was palpable.

The woman at the well was absolutely right when she said that Jews and Samaritans did not associate with each other. They had no dealings with each other at any time or any place. They did not worship together in the same temple. They did not live together in the same provinces, towns or neighborhoods. They did not socialize or eat together. They did not attend the same schools. They did not share *anything* in common. The resulting hostile segregation was so great that if a Samaritan person and a Jewish person were walking on a sunny day and the Samaritan's shadow crossed the Jew's shadow, the Jewish person considered himself unclean. That's how much they avoided each other! They stayed as far away as possible.

So why was this Jew talking to her? Sam had good reason to wonder.

A MAN'S WORLD

In addition to having to live with the stigma of being a Samaritan, Sam was born a woman. Women in her society were considered to be property—you belonged either to your father or to your husband. Even children had greater status in society than women. The primary purpose of a woman in that culture was to have children—preferably male children. That's why the Bible is full of stories like those of Hannah, Sarah and Elizabeth—women who cried out to God in anguish, begging to give birth to a child. Women were considered cursed by God and had no real worth in society if they could not bear children. Men felt themselves to be fortunate and blessed because they were not born female. In the Jerusalem temple during worship, devout men would often address God with a prayer that said, "Lord, I thank you I was not born a slave, a Gentile [some translations say 'imbecile'] or a woman!" This was not intended to be a slur; rather, it was considered a genuine act of worship in the presence of God.

If you were a *Samaritan* woman among Jews in that day, the disgrace was even greater. "A Jewish regulation of A.D. 65-66 warned that one could never count on the ritual purity of Samaritan women since they were menstruants from their cradle!" This decree was based upon an Old Testament Scripture that called for every woman to be kept apart from the general population during the time of her menstrual cycle. (I know this is a hard topic for most men to even think about, let alone read about in the Bible! Just imagine never being able to have sex with your wife—that is what this law meant.) Leviticus 15:19-23 says,

> When a woman has her regular flow of blood, the impurity of her monthly period will last seven days, and anyone who touches her will be unclean till evening. Anything she lies on during her period will be unclean, and anything she sits on will be unclean. Whoever touches her bed must wash his clothes and bathe with water, and he will be unclean till evening. Whoever touches anything she sits on must wash his clothes and bathe with water, and he will be unclean till evening. Whether it is the bed or anything she was sitting on, when anyone touches it, he will be unclean till evening.

If you were a Jewish woman, then, your times of segregation from the community ended once you were no longer menstruating. However, if you were a Samaritan woman you were declared a "perpetual menstruate"—meaning there was never a time when you were not unclean. From the time you were a little girl until you were an old, gray-haired woman, you were never clean—never good enough to be touched, never acceptable. For seven days a week, 365 days of the year, you were seen as filthy, dirty, unclean. There was never a day that you were clean enough to sit next to a Jewish person. Anything you sat on or drank from immediately became unclean and had to broken, burned or discarded. No one could eat after you or shake your hand, because to do so would cause them to become immediately unclean.

Can you imagine what it must do to a person's self-esteem and self-image to be told every day of her life that something is wrong with her? That she doesn't measure up? That she's not good enough? That she is dirty, unworthy or defective? When there is no social source of positive images to counteract these pervasive negative messages, over time this type of persistent, cultural assault creates a "hole in your soul." Before long, even the strongest people start doubting themselves and begin looking for love in all the wrong places—simply trying to fill the emptiness inside.

As a black woman growing up in American society, I understand this. I know what it's like to live in an environment where there is little that validates you or affirms your worth. The images that I see on television do not affirm my beauty as an African American woman. When I was growing up and watched the Miss America Pageant on television, I never imagined that the next Miss America would look like me. I didn't even expect a black woman to place! Beauty was for white girls, or for black girls who looked as close to white as possible. I know what it's like to drown in a sea of negative images of your people group in the media and in popular culture.

As I grew up in a working-class urban neighborhood, my parents regularly gave me messages trying to counter the negative impact the culture was having on my self-esteem. My mother would say things like "You can't be as good as; you have to be better than"—meaning as a black person I would have to be twice as good as my white counterparts if I was to succeed. She would also look me right in the eye and say, "You're as good as anybody else," as if trying to convince me—and maybe even herself—

that this was true. Not all parents have to talk to their children in this way. I now know that sociologists and psychologists call this "racial and ethnic socialization." My mother was trying to make up for the toll that society was taking on my soul.

THE HOLES IN OUR SOULS

I relate to the Samaritan woman because she also grew up in a society where there was very little affirmation and validation of her worth as a woman or as an ethnic person. I believe that after a while she developed "a hole in her soul." It could be that she lacked the nurture and affirmation she so desperately needed and eventually she began to look for love in all the wrong places. Maybe she was thirsty for love, for someone who would affirm her and validate her and touch her—someone who didn't think of her as dirty, unclean and defiled. So perhaps she tried to fill the hole in her soul with romantic relationships. She wasn't a bad person. She was a thirsty person—just like you and me. She needed validation. She needed nurture. She needed affection. All of us do. Human beings are born needing nurture and personal care. Scientists have proven that babies will fail to thrive if they do not get love and attention, even if all of their physical needs are met. As people made in the image of God, we are relational beings, and we need to be in caring, life-giving relationships.

I think my friend Sam tried to fill the hole in her soul by getting married. She looked for a man who would say, "I love you and I want to spend the rest of my life with you—I want to marry you."

That may be her story. What's yours? What messages have you received over time that have caused you to doubt your unique worth as a person made in the image of God? We human beings live in a broken and fallen world. We all make mistakes and none of our relationships are perfect. It could be that some of your early, primary relationships didn't provide all you needed to develop a healthy self-concept. Then there are the not-good-enough messages we are constantly bombarded with through the media and popular culture. It's hard to receive subliminal negative messages on a daily basis—you're not good enough, you're not pretty enough, you're not thin enough, rich enough, smart enough—and not be affected by them on some level, conscious or unconscious.

How are you trying to fill the hole in your soul? Maybe your dad wanted a boy and got a girl instead, and now you find yourself struggling with sexual issues and trying to find someone who will love you for who you are. Maybe your mother was afraid that you would repeat the mistakes of her past and was overly protective or critical of you, and you have become a high achiever, a perfectionist or a workaholic, trying to prove yourself. Still other people are trying to fill the hole in their soul through food, shopping, drugs, alcohol or gambling—trying to feel secure and successful if only for a short while. It could be that English is not your primary language and now that you live in an English-speaking society your speech is used to judge your intelligence, level of sophistication or ability to perform well in school or on the job. You have learned to go along with the system, but it has taken its toll, and you have developed a hole in your soul.

I'm not sure what messages you have received from your family of origin or the culture around you, but I do know that there is a little bit of my friend Sam's story in all of us. At first we may have thought that we have nothing in common with this woman who has been characterized as a person of ill-repute with low moral standards. However, all of us are shaped by the context in which we live, and our stories are shaped by our cultural background. Having looked more closely, we have found that the Samaritan woman's story is very much like our own story. She was looking for and needed what we all need—someone or something that is real and lasting, that will help us to make sense of our life and give us a greater purpose. That is true for the corporate executive in a high-rise building, it's true for the woman at the well, and it's true for us. This is the collective human narrative, and it is into this story that Jesus enters.

BEGIN WITH A DIVINE MANDATE

But he had to go through Samaria.

JOHN 4:4

One day after I moved to Chicago, I was reading the local newspaper and learned about a radical Catholic priest named Father Michael Pfleger who lives on the south side of the city. He was regularly making headlines for painting over billboards in the primarily African American community where he lives and pastors a prominent church called St. Sabina. This south side community was the birthplace of the Irish parade, but now, due in part to white flight, it faces some of the great inner-city challenges that are found in many other urban areas around the country.

Father Pfleger and his church were concerned about the high number of billboards that targeted children of their community with destructive images and messages. Pfleger knew that certain products are marketed very specifically to residents of the inner city. The health hazards of beer and hard liquor are serious enough, let alone the negative social and emotional impact of having such products advertised on almost every street corner in one's neighborhood. Father Pfleger and the members of his church were particularly concerned about the children of their community. A large number of the negative billboards were located close to schools, playgrounds and recreational centers. Father Pfleger and his congregation knew that such unhelpful messages were having a corrosive effect on the collective psyche of the people who had to see them every day, and it was especially important to protect young, impressionable minds. Black children who grow up on a steady diet of images associating glamour and success with alcohol and tobacco cannot help but develop a negative view of themselves.

Father Pfleger requested that the sponsors of these billboards respect his community and take them down. They refused. So out of frustration and love for the people he served, a white priest picked up a can of red paint and a paintbrush and began taking matters into his own hands.

Later I learned that Father Pfleger was brought into court on criminal charges. His defense was that under the circumstances a drastic action had to be taken—this is called a "necessity defense." It was explained that he and his church had gathered information about the effects of the proliferation of the billboards in his community to present to the companies that manufacture the products. He tried to discuss the problem directly with the manufacturers and the ad agencies that create the billboards, to reach an amicable solution. These attempts were made over an extended period, giving the companies ample time to respond, to no avail. Pfleger's legal team documented the destructive nature of the products in question and provided a full history of the attempts Father Pfleger and his congregation had made to get the companies to take self-corrective action. It was only after all of these avenues had been exhausted that this priest felt he had to take more direct action personally to remedy the situation. The jury found him not guilty.

COMPELLED BY GOD

In our Scripture text, what appears to be a small detail actually encompasses an important truth: Jesus also was compelled and *had* to do something that others would not do. Just like Father Pfleger, who had to do something to address injustices and inequities in his community, Jesus had a mandate from God that compelled him to bring the ministry of reconciliation to the Samaritans.

So the story of his encounter with the woman at the well begins with a "necessity defense." John 4:4 says, "[Now Jesus] had to go through Samaria." The word *had* seems to imply that it was necessary for Jesus to go through Samaria—that he had no other choice. However, on a cultural, social, political or religious level *this was not true*. Many Jews of Jesus' day simply refused to go through Samaria.

Palestine was divided into three parts: Galilee in the north, Judea in the south and Samaria in the middle. It is likely that Jesus set out from Capernaum, traveled to the remaining villages of Galilee as far as Samaria, and then passed through the small province of Samaria. The Samaritans occupied land that was situated between Jerusalem and Galilee, so that to go from one to the other, it might seem natural to pass through Samaria. Yet most Jews avoided Samaria like the plague. They steered clear of it by taking a dangerous road full of hairpin turns where thieves could ambush, beat and rob them. An unsuspecting traveler on this curving road could not see the thugs waiting around the bend. But some Jews preferred to risk the perils of this treacherous and circuitous road rather than to be caught dead in Samaria. One reason the story of the "good Samaritan" in Luke 10:25-37 is so compelling is that it demonstrates the power of compassion in the face of hatred and alienation. The Samaritan stops to help a Jewish man who has likely been injured in the course of taking the perilous road out of a bigoted refusal to go through the place where the Samaritans live. Had he been conscious, the Jewish man might have spat in his rescuer's face!

AVOIDING SAMARIA

We, too, have our ways of getting around "Samaria." City planners design freeways and choose locations for malls that allow us to avoid certain people and neighborhoods. The news media can give us selective coverage and only report on certain events. Individually we can refuse to travel; we can stay isolated within our own country and thus avoid certain nationalities or cultural groups. When we do travel, we can choose destinations that allow us to remain tourists and never be touched by the struggles of the people who live there. Churches, companies and organizations can choose to locate their houses of worship or headquarters in places that keep them far from certain people. Employment opportunities can be advertised only among friends or in selective publications that keep certain people in the "club" and others out. These are some of the ways we avoid "Samaria" and close our eyes to the real pain of people right in our backyard.

Recent U.S. Census reports suggests that all U.S. communities—urban, suburban and rural—are currently faced with problems that were historically thought to be isolated to certain groups of people. Unemployment, crime, drugs, poverty and homelessness are now endemic in many communities around the country. "The enduring social and fiscal challenges for cities stemming from high poverty are increasingly shared by their suburbs. . . . In 1999 large cities and their suburbs had nearly equal numbers of poor individuals, but by 2005 the suburban poor outnumbered their city counterparts by at least 1 million." Even if we have chosen a "safe" neighborhood, there may be people living right next door or nearby who are facing economically uncertain times—but we don't know it because we have closed our eyes to their reality and found a way, consciously or unconsciously, to avoid Samaria.

Why did Jesus *have* to go through Samaria? What compelled him? What was his motivation? Why was it necessary for Jesus to do what no other Jew had to do? We know that it was not a geographic necessity: another road was available. Neither was it for religious, sociopolitical or cultural reasons. There was a deep religious divide between the Jews and Samaritans, and this resulted in their social, political and cultural aversion to each other. At one point the Old Testament describes the religious practices of the Samaritans by saying, "They worshiped the LORD but also served their own gods, after the manner of the nations from among whom they had been carried away" (2 Kings 17:33). Later "the Jews, after their return from Babylon, set about rebuilding their temple. The Samaritans offered to aid them. The Jews, however, perceiving that it was not from a love of true religion, but that they might obtain a part of the favors granted to the Jews by Cyrus, rejected their offer. The consequence was that a state of long and bitter animosity arose between them and the Jews." As we have seen, their religious differences grew into a cultural and sociopolitical chasm that was rooted in years of suspicion and contempt and was evident in their mutual segregation.

Jesus certainly could have avoided Samaria, just as most Jews did. However, he seemed to be compelled by a power greater than his political, social, cultural and religious context. Hebrews tells us that Jesus quoted Psalm 40 to declare that his purpose and motivation was different:

> Sacrifices and offerings you have not desired,
>   but a body you have prepared for me;
> in burnt offerings and sin offerings
>   you have taken no pleasure.
> Then I said, "See, God, I have come to do your will, O God."
> (Hebrews 10:5-7)

CALLED TO BE RECONCILERS

I believe that Jesus "had to" go through Samaria because he was compelled by the Father's heart. There was a divine mandate at work in his life—a divine directive, purpose or calling that caused him to live differently than the world around him. He came to do God's will. This was a necessity for Jesus, and it is also a necessity for us. We have a similar mandate—a word that literally means to "put into one's hand, command or entrust." In 2 Corinthians 5:18-20 the apostle Paul makes this quite clear when he says, "All this is from God, who reconciled us to himself through Christ, and has given us the ministry of reconciliation; that is, in Christ God was reconciling the world to himself, not counting their trespasses against them, and entrusting the message of reconciliation to us. So we are ambassadors for Christ, since God is making his appeal through us; we entreat you on behalf of Christ, be reconciled to God."

We are called to be reconcilers. This is our divine mandate. The message of reconciliation and the message of evangelism are therefore one and the same: Jesus Christ died to reconcile us back to God, and in embracing that reconciliation we are reconciled to each other. Both things were accomplished at the same time, in the same act of salvation. Our mandate and calling is to live differently from the world around us so that all people—regardless of their differences—might be drawn into a divine relationship with God and each other as a new act of creation.

This is what true, life-changing evangelism is, and it begins with God—in the heart of God. Compelled by the love of God for us and for the world, we choose to follow a divine mandate to cross gender lines, racial barriers, denominational divides, political affiliations, age separations and class distinctions. This is not a *good* idea—it's a *God* idea!

We receive our divine mandate by listening to God. We must learn to listen afresh to the voice of God—to ask God for direction and then to distinguish God's voice from the clamor of the culture and the crowds around us. One of the most powerful questions in Scripture is "What then should we do?" (Luke 3:10). What should we do to restore our believability as credible witnesses of the gospel? What should we do to cross cultures and build bridges in a world looking for a way to end wars and bring peace? What should we do to compellingly engage the culture around us? Once we prayerfully ask such a simply profound question, we are provided with a divine mandate, and then it is no longer an option to do nothing.

Our human efforts will be short-lived if we don't have a divine reason for doing what we do. To be a credible witness of the gospel, we must begin with a mandate from God. This divine mandate will bring us in contact with people like the Samaritan woman—people who are unlike us: people who don't look like us, who may be from a different racial, ethnic or religious group, who may speak a different language, be of a different gender or come from another country around the world. They are people whom God loves and wants to reach through us. Although they may not know it, they have a divine appointment with God, and we are being used as evangelists to bring them the good news that they are persons of unsurpassable worth and are profoundly loved by God.

A DIVINE APPOINTMENT

This is why Jesus "had" to go to Samaria. A mandate from God compelled him to go—to *be* the good news that would affirm the dignity and worth of the Samaritan woman. This validation and affirmation completely caught my friend Sam off guard. Although she deeply needed it and longed for it, she was not expecting it. That's the interesting thing about Jesus. We can never know for certain when and where he will show up or when we might have a divine appointment with him. Many people assume that Jesus shows up only in places where we expect him to be, like church, at religious functions or at holy times like Sunday morning or Easter. Since we expect him on such occasions, many of us spruce ourselves up and put on our "religious selves" so we can appear more acceptable to God. However, what the woman at the well discovered is that Jesus actually shows up in the most unlikely places—in places and on days when we least expect him.

My friend Sam was at the well, and she didn't expect anyone else to be there. That's why she went at twelve noon. It was customary for women to go to the well early in the morning or late in the evening when the sun was not beating down, but my friend Sam wanted to be alone. As a woman with a bad reputation, she preferred to avoid other women, who shunned her and made her feel more ashamed of herself—like a social outcast. She was tired of people whispering behind her back, and she was tired of the self-righteous stares.

When she came to the well and found Jesus—a Jew—wanting to engage her in conversation, she was shocked! She responded somewhat indignantly and defensively, in essence saying, "What are you doing talking to me? Don't you know my ethnicity? Doesn't that bother you? You are a Jew and I am a Samaritan woman. Jews and Samaritans don't associate with each other. What's more, if you knew who I really am, you would know that most people don't want to talk to me or be with me. Don't you know who I am? Don't you know what I've done? I've got secrets and I've made mistakes. Don't you know my reputation? Don't you know that I'm not a holy person?"

Isn't that our greatest fear—that if people really knew who we are on the inside they wouldn't love us or want to be with us? Maybe you feel like my friend Sam—Jesus shouldn't be talking to you. You're sure that if Jesus knew the things you do in secret, the pornographic websites you visit on the computer, or the self-hatred you harbor on the inside while trying to mask it with makeup, a nice car or pretty clothes on the outside, he really wouldn't want to be with you. Maybe you struggle with a sense of inadequacy or you have difficulty trusting. It might be that you are fearful and often feel cynical. But Jesus said to my friend Sam, and he says to you and me, "You're exactly the person I came here to see. I know you, and you do not repulse me. No matter what you've done, what society says about you or how distant you are from me, I love you unconditionally, and you're exactly who I want to talk to. I came here specifically to be with you."

My friend Sam was minding her own business, involved in her normal activities, when Jesus showed up at the most unlikely time and place. He has a way of doing that. Like the woman at the well, you will discover that Jesus doesn't wait just for special, religious occasions. He shows up during the normal stuff of life—on your job, at the grocery store, at the laundry while you're washing your clothes, in the cafeteria or while you're watching a movie. When we least expect it, Jesus shows up and we discover, much to our surprise, that we are scheduled for a divine appointment with God.

It was a divine mandate that caused Jesus to seek and find an unsuspecting woman who desperately needed to know she was loved. It is this same divine mandate that compels his followers to model the gospel wherever they are so that others might discover how much God loves them.

JESUS SHOWS UP ON CAMPUS

It was on a Wednesday afternoon in 1974 when I discovered that I had a divine appointment with God. I was beginning my sophomore year as a student at Rutgers University in New Brunswick, New Jersey. My freshman year had been disastrous academically. During that year I had used my independence and newfound freedom to party and raise my social standing on campus with the attractive and popular guys. It worked, but I almost partied my way right out of college—I was placed on academic probation. I started my sophomore year with a determination to do better.

One day as I was walking down the hall toward the women's bathroom on my dormitory floor, I heard "church music" coming from someone's room. Now I had been raised in a churchgoing and religious family. As we got ready for church each Sunday morning, my mother would tune the radio to the local station that aired the *Gospel Cavalcade* program, and church music would fill our house. But we almost never played gospel music any other day of the week. So it seemed extremely odd to me that someone in my college dorm would be playing gospel music on a *Wednesday*—it felt like the wrong day! I became curious and intrigued.

I peeked into the room the music was coming from and saw that no one was there. When I went into the bathroom, though, I found the gospel-music lover standing in front of the mirror combing her hair. Her name was Margaret Alma Blackwell, and she was the most beautiful Christian woman I had ever seen. I enjoyed church and assumed that someday I would become a Christian—if for no other reason than to avoid hell—it was definitely not something I planned to do until I was much older! But now standing in the bathroom, looking at Margaret in the mirror and later watching her live an impressive and attractive Christian life, I began to desire what she had.

I noticed, for example, that guys on our dormitory floor watched their language around her and avoided profanity. They didn't use the same restraint around my other girlfriends and me. I wanted guys to treat me with respect the way they treated Margaret. She carried herself with a sense of dignity and quiet strength. She was not swayed by peer pressure or by what other people thought about her. She was free to be herself. Although I looked as if I was self-assured, the truth was that I struggled with low self-esteem and tried to compensate for it by getting people to like me. I had the "disease to please," and it was causing me to make bad choices. Deep inside I longed to have the confidence and character I saw in Margaret. As a result of the lifestyle of this young woman, who followed God's mandate to live differently from the world around her, I saw a credible witness of the gospel that drew me into a divine appointment.

There are many thirsty people like me on college campuses, in churches, in organizations and communities who need to meet credible witnesses of the gospel. Jesus *had* to go through Samaria, and so do we. We must follow his example if we are to gain credibility with people of different cultures, ethnicities and nationalities and if we are going to reach people who have been beat up or marginalized by society or by the church.

When was the last time you *had to* do something that you felt called to do by God? When have you had a conviction in your soul that compelled you to move forward even when your peers didn't have a similar desire? Although it is not always socially acceptable, not always popular, we are called to the ministry of reconciliation. We have been entrusted with a specific message—that Jesus Christ died to reconcile us to God and to each other. The two things were accomplished at the same time, in the same act of salvation. This is real Christianity, and to preach anything less is not the gospel. We represent a new reality—the kingdom of God, a new world order where diverse people live together in peace, love and justice

because of Jesus. This is our story, and we have a mandate to tell it—
sometimes using words, sometimes just walking into the "wrong" neighborhood or standing at a mirror combing our hair.

That's why Father Michael Pfleger's story is so important to me. It demonstrates the integral connection between evangelism and reconciliation
and gives us a collective model of a credible witness.

Let's look more closely at the divine mandate that compelled Father
Pfleger and his church to act. First, Father Mike has lived in his community on the south side of Chicago for more than thirty years. This is not
just the community where he pastors; this is also his home, his neighborhood. Our credibility is established over time as we live with the people
we seek to reach. Father Pfleger has proven himself to be a credible witness of the gospel by living and suffering with the people in his community—most of whom are different from him racially, culturally and socio-
economically, but the issues that concern them about their community
are also the issues that concern him.

Father Pfleger and his congregation were specifically concerned about
protecting children. In court, this garnered support from a broader community of people that transcended race, ethnicity or class, because all
people and parents can relate to the need to protect children regardless of
their ethnicity or where they live.

Because a radical Catholic priest had a divine mandate and was willing
to take risks to save children, many people—including me—heard and
saw a credible witness to the gospel. I learned that when Christians come
to the defense of people who are vulnerable and have been wronged and
mistreated, it shows our credibility. Something has to be done, and God
calls us to get involved. St. Sabina is a thriving church with many parish-
ioners who have been drawn to Christ because of the courageous witness
of this priest and his church, who have a divine mandate to make a difference in their community and in the world.

ENGAGE IN
INTENTIONAL INTERACTION

*So he came to a Samaritan city called Sychar, near the plot of
ground that Jacob had given to his son Joseph. Jacob's well was
there, and Jesus, tired out by his journey, was sitting by the well.*

JOHN 4:5-6

For years I have been saying that I want to learn to speak Spanish. Although I have a basic facility with the language, the truth is that my ability to communicate to Spanish speakers is limited, and I understand only about 40 percent of what is being said to me—and that's on a good day! As long as I stay in the United States, I can always fall back on my English skills and ability to influence people with my persuasive personality. In this country I know what jokes to tell in order to build rapport with my audience. I understand the cultural cues that allow me to accurately interpret my context, and I'm aware of many of the subtle expectations that are associated with being a minister in most Christian denominations. The United States is home; I am comfortable here, and I have learned how to succeed in this context.

One day I mentioned my desire to learn Spanish to Pastors Gamaliel and Nicole Aguado, a couple who planted churches in Mexico. To my surprise, they challenged me to be intentional by going with them to Mexico for two weeks. The purpose of this trip was to visit congregations and encourage their spiritual growth and to provide biblical and ministerial training to church leaders.

I decided to accept the invitation. I assumed that I would be going as an observer and I would try to be as helpful as I could. However, I was shocked when I learned that Pastors Gamaliel and Nicole had scheduled me to preach in churches and to lead women's seminars in Ixtapa, Zihuatanejo, Morelia and Uruapán! They said that if I was serious about learning the language, I would have to put myself intentionally in situations where I would have to use it. So I agreed and promptly embarked on a crash course in Spanish to prepare. Nicole met with me regularly to help get me ready for the trip, to inform me about the cities we would visit and to pray. Still, when the time came to leave I was scared: I felt woefully unprepared and totally unready for this experience.

In Mexico I learned how it feels not to be in control. Simple social interactions required great effort for me. Greeting people after church or going out for a meal together was hard work. Small children could communicate better than I could. One day when I was at a hotel I thought, *If there were a fire and an announcement were made over the intercom for everyone to evacuate, I might be the only person left in this hotel watching television because I didn't understand the message!* However, as time went on, I learned to trust and depend on other people. Pastors Gamaliel and Nicole encouraged me to say as much as I could in Spanish without their help, but when I needed them they were always there to bail me out. Nicole was my interpreter, and she did an excellent job of translating what I said in English to relevant concepts in Spanish. Someone commented that we worked together like a cufflink in a shirt.

It was an incredible experience for me. The people were extremely gracious and receptive. In addition to learning to speak Spanish, I learned about the divide that exists between people from different social classes in Mexico. Their cultural reconciliation issues are different from those that exist in the United States. In a setting where I was completely out of my comfort zone, it was amazing to watch God use me to help women divided by sharp class distinctions—rich, working-class and poor—begin to come together as sisters in Jesus Christ because of the gospel. All of this happened because I was forced to be intentional.

When Jesus sat down by a well in Samaria, he was being intentional. John 4:6 tells us where Jesus chose to sit and why: "Jacob's well was there, and Jesus, tired out by his journey, was sitting by the well. It was about noon." He was hot and thirsty, having traveled a far distance. The capital city of Samaria was "situated about 15 miles to the northwest of the city of Shechem or Sychar and about 40 miles to the north of Jerusalem. Sychar or Shechem was also a city within the limits of Samaria." The well Jesus sat by is reported to have been about eighty-five to one hundred feet deep. It had been cut through solid limestone rock and was covered with a large stone. It is commonly referred to as "Jacob's well" because tradition says that he dug it or that it was near the land he had given to his son Joseph at the foot of Mount Gerizim. Today this well is dry.

That well was a likely place for Jesus to meet a Samaritan woman. In that culture the arduous job and responsibility of carrying water to and from a community well fell to women. This is still the case in many countries around the world today. While visiting Kenya, I saw women and young girls carrying huge jars on their heads to and from the river. I saw how very difficult this task is and how much physical strength it requires. I watched in amazement as men helped women hoist huge jars onto their head and these powerful women balanced this cargo with dignity and grace—sometimes while also carrying a baby on their back!

Carrying water was women's work. So when Jesus sat down by that well, he must have been expecting to meet a Samaritan woman. The odds were in favor of it! Generally, however, women did not go to the well at noon as was mentioned earlier. Only a marginalized woman would appear at that time of day.

LEAVING OUR COMFORT ZONE

Often when we want to reach people with the gospel, we ask them to come to us. We plan special evangelistic events and invite them. We might ask them to attend a conference or visit our church. This is not wrong to do, but Jesus seems to be giving us an alternative strategy. So maybe we need to ask ourselves, *How do we get more Christians to go where the people are?* What will it take to get us to leave our comfort zone and intentionally go to places where we will meet people who are different from us?

Jesus left Judea, and on his way back to Galilee he went through Samaria. He left the place where he knew the customs, spoke the language and liked the food. He left the place where he was comfortable and went to a place where he was not in control. This kind of evangelism will win credibility with people all around the world. It will show that we understand and take seriously their context and their reality. But it requires that we leave our comfort zone and go to places where we do not speak the language, where we are not in control and where people are not necessarily impressed with our academic degrees or other qualifications. It could be that this is the more powerful witness—that we take the risk to go to where people are instead of asking them to come to us.

A very practical and moving example of this is demonstrated in the life of a Christian African American woman named Doris. She and her family bought a very nice home in an affluent suburban community, where they are in the minority. When she moved into the neighborhood she felt isolated from her neighbors. No one reached out to her and her family to make them feel welcome. No one was hostile, but everyone kept to themselves. Doris realized that this was typical of many American communities today: Often people are too busy and don't really have time to get to know their neighbors. People may wave to each other, but rarely do they speak or have time to interact. Doris recalls that the only visitors her family would get when they first moved in were the local police, who regularly drove by casting suspicious looks, shining bright lights on their property and trying to see what was going on.

Instead of becoming bitter or withdrawn, Doris decided to intentionally get to know her neighbors. She prayed about what to do and felt that God led her to "invest in her community." So she decided to take the initiative. Her major goal was to build a bridge to the community and build relationships. She joined an organization for women that raised money for worthy causes in the community and surrounding county. This group is highly visible, participating in local parades and community events. After a year of working with the group, Doris was asked to be on the board; later she served as the treasurer for three years. Through this involvement she became more visible and active in the community, and people began to know her and trust her. She established herself as a credible witness of the gospel.

Over the years, Doris has had many opportunities to share her faith with people in her community. They have watched her life and have seen how she conducts herself in meetings and social events. They noticed differences about her, such as the fact that she doesn't drink or swear. Yet she was different without condemning others. Some people became curious and asked her questions about Christianity. Some took her into their confidence and asked her to pray for them and their families. She listened with empathy as they talked about difficulties with their children, family brokenness or serious health problems. She learned that many people who look wealthy on the outside have deep needs on the inside and don't know whom they can trust.

Doris has become a credible witness for the kingdom of God because she was intentional. Today she works at a local elementary school, providing academic support for sixth-, seventh- and eighth-grade students. In this role she often has the opportunity to tell her story. She has helped European American children to understand some of what it was like for her growing up in the segregated South in the 1950s. Through her they have gotten a glimpse of the social reality of discrimination and diversity in America. Some of them have written her letters letting her know what a difference she has made to their understanding.

When asked about her evangelism, Doris said, "It's all about relationships. It's about getting to know people and letting them get to know you. If I can open my heart so that people can see that there are people who genuinely care, then perhaps it will open a door for someone else. I'm glad that I've been able to make a difference."

The people that Doris intentionally reached out to were not foreigners who lived across the globe from her. Instead they were people who lived right across the street. This is what distinguishes this type of intentional interaction from a traditional call to world missions. The first place in which we are called to be a credible witness is "Samaria," the community or group of people nearby where we have a prior history and some level of relationship. Like Doris, we go without predetermined methods or strategies but directed by God. We pray and remain open to the possibility of God's using us in a transformative way while we are there.

FINDING OUR SAMARIA

I believe that God is calling all of us to make a difference, but to do this we will have to be intentional about leaving behind what is safe and familiar to us. We will have to put ourselves in places where we are not in control, and that make us uncomfortable. For most of us this place will be our "Samaria." Metaphorically this is the place that we'd prefer to avoid. It's the place that we find creative ways to bypass. Samaria is the place where we are not in power. It's the place where we don't like the people; we don't speak their language or understand their customs. We feel out of place. It may be that we've had a bad experience and are somewhat frightened of the people there. Whatever the reason, we really don't want to be with them.

Where is your "Samaria"? Who is it that you avoid? How do you avoid their turf? Why do you avoid it? Generally, Samaria is relatively close to us but we feel alienated and distant from the people there. It could be that your Samaria is a table in the cafeteria where people of certain ethnic groups eat together. Maybe your Samaria is a street corner near your church where homeless people regularly beg for money. Perhaps you feel most uncomfortable in a store or business establishment where the people don't speak your language. You may find that Samaria is with estranged members of your own family. Samaria might be the place where young, rowdy teenagers hang out. It could be the place where many gay and lesbian people live. Samaria can be a poor urban neighborhood, a prison on the outskirts of town in rural America or an ethnic enclave in a suburban community. Wherever it is, Samaria is a place where people are not in power and feel marginalized by us. It's the place where people who differ from us gather, and if we intentionally sit down by the "wells" there, we just might have a life-changing encounter.

There are many ways that we can intentionally go to Samaria. There are urban and global projects for college and graduate students to participate in. We could choose to join a church that serves a community that we desire to reach. We could intentionally support an ethnic-specific establishment with our business. A Christian organization could intentionally build or buy property in an underresourced community and use it for ministry. I know of many Christians who are buying homes in urban neighborhoods and living there as witnesses while they serve the needs of the poor in their community together. This is a wonderful model of how to change a community from the inside out. A college that I consult with intentionally started a multiethnic gospel choir. This choir tours the United States, visiting racially different communities and serving as "goodwill ambassadors" for the school. They have become so popular that now an admissions counselor accompanies them with a promotional DVD highlighting the diversity efforts of the school. They are experiencing great success, evidenced by an increase in their recruitment and retention of ethnic minority students.

MORE THAN A METHOD

Jesus demonstrates what it looks like to intentionally reach across the human boundaries of culture, class, ethnicity, religion and gender. As his followers, we too are called to be willing to cross the cultural and social boundaries that have separated us from Samaria. This will not be easy. It is much easier to stay with our own group. But if we want to pursue God's kingdom, we will need to be open to changing the way we think about things—to view life differently. To do this we have to be open to going to Samaria.

This is much more than a method for doing crosscultural evangelism. It is about being in the right place at the right time and learning to be open and obedient to God's leading and direction. It's about God using us in transformative moments when and where we least expect it. Our willingness to go beyond typical boundaries is an evangelistic statement in and of itself. It is to *that* place that we are called to go. We obey God and go to sit down by "wells" in Samaria to intentionally interact with diverse people, because this is the place where important events can happen that can transform lives, communities and nations.

4

RELINQUISH POWER
AND EMBRACE NEED

Jesus said to her, "Give me a drink."

JOHN 4:7

I was in high school in the early 1970s, a few years after the assassination of Dr. Martin Luther King Jr. and during the turbulent times of the civil rights era in the United States. I can remember seeing race riots break out in school and white students being beaten in the hallways. A white male student who lived near my home was thrown from a second-floor window. One teacher, Mr. Nast, a very nice permanent substitute, was beaten up in his classroom. That was a terrible day! These were very tense and volatile times, and it was in this racially tense atmosphere that I got my first summer job.

I was hired as a counselor in a summer camp program in Pennington, New Jersey. This recreational and tutorial program brought children from urban schools in Trenton, New Jersey, to Pennington, an affluent rural community. The program helped these children to improve their basic academic skills and exposed them to music, art and fun activities like riding horses, playing tennis and swimming. Twelve counselors were hired to staff the program. Six of the counselors were African Americans from Trenton, and six were white Americans from Pennington. Two of the white counselors were the sons of the program's founder, Dorothy Katz. The counselors were asked to arrive one week before the children did. On the first day of orientation, all the counselors self-segregated along racial lines. The African American counselors felt intimidated by the affluence of Pennington, and we decided that the philosophical premise of the program was flawed. We felt that it was unfair to expose poor black children to experiences that highlighted their poverty and could not be duplicated in their home communities. To express our displeasure and to intimidate the white people in the program, all of the African Americans came the next day dressed in cultural clothing and wearing Afro hairstyles. We tried to look as militant and menacing as we could. The white counselors were afraid of us and kept far away. The atmosphere was tense, and neither group made any effort toward dialogue or reconciliation.

Mrs. Katz saw that her program was in jeopardy of being destroyed before it ever got started! She decided that she had to build a team out of this racially divided group. To do this, she contacted an adventure learning organization and instructed all twelve counselors to come the next day prepared to go camping. She arranged for us to be taken into the woods for a wilderness survival weekend.

We were driven to an undisclosed location and given food rations for two days. A man dressed in hiking gear met our team and took us into a very dense, remote wilderness area. I was afraid and felt out of control in this unfamiliar territory. I kept to myself and didn't even try to participate with the rest of the group. Having brought my own snacks, I refused to eat the freeze-dried rations that were given to us. I was not a good team player!

On the next day we had to climb a steep rock face to reach the place to be picked up. I had never been camping before and did not have proper camping gear, hiking boots or climbing attire. After several failed attempts at trying to scale the face of the rock, I almost gave up, exhausted. My fingers were bleeding and my legs were cut and bruised. I needed help.

One of the counselors, Danny Katz, saw me in crisis. Everyone else had gone on ahead. Instead of leaving me, he reached down his hand, stretching to grab me, and he pulled me up with all his strength to the top of that rock.

When I was safely on the rock, our eyes met; I looked him right in the face. We didn't speak, but in that moment I saw him in a new way. I was too young and dumb—and probably arrogant—to know how to properly thank him, but I knew that I could never hate him again. I had had a real need, and he reached for me and met it. As a result he was no longer just a "white boy" to me. He was a real person with a name—Danny Katz—and I have never forgotten him.

That was the day that my reconciliation journey began. I wasn't a Christian yet, but God used my need and Danny's response to start the process of transforming my life.

TIRED AND THIRSTY FROM THE JOURNEY

The interaction between Jesus and the Samaritan woman also begins with a real need. In John 4:6-8 we learn that Jesus was tired and thirsty when he reached Samaria:

> Jesus, tired out by his journey, was sitting by the well. It was about noon.
>
> A Samaritan woman came to draw water, and Jesus said to her, "Give me a drink." (His disciples had gone to the city to buy food.)

When Jesus sat down by the well he had an immediate problem—nothing to draw water with. His companions couldn't help him, because they were gone into town to get food. So when the Samaritan woman arrived with a jar and a means to get water from the well, Jesus asked her for a drink. He really needed her help.

His conversation with the Samaritan woman begins with Jesus' accepting and acknowledging his real need for something that the woman has. He didn't make this up to start an evangelistic conversation with her. He was not making small talk or casting about for a clever, evangelistic thing to say. He was really thirsty, and he really needed a drink of water.

Remember, Jesus was traveling by foot from Judea to Galilee under the hot Middle Eastern desert sun. It was high noon, the hottest time of the day, and the sun was beating down on him and his fellow travelers. He arrived in this scorching heat to a town named Sychar. As noted earlier, it was located near the capital city of Samaria, which had once been large and splendid. This beautiful city was "built by Omri, who purchased 'the hill Samaria' of Shemer, for two talents of silver, equal in value to 792 British pounds. . . . (He) built the city on the hill, and called it, after the name of Shemer, Samaria (1 Kings 16:24). Omri was king of Israel (925 B.C.), and he made this city the capital of his kingdom. The city was built on a pleasant and fertile hill, and surrounded by a rich valley, with a circle of hills beyond." The city was the crown of the region. Having restored the city in 21 B.C. after it was destroyed, Herod the Great called it Sebaste (Latin Augusta), in honor of the emperor Augustus. The people of this region thus had a history of elevation and decline. While they were considered to be "less" by the Jews, it is likely they cultivated a sense of cultural pride.

When the woman approaches the well, Jesus does not address her from a position of formal power. He does not approach her as a "sinner." He could have easily demonstrated his spiritual insight and prophetic power by launching into the topic of her past failed relationships and sinful lifestyle. When she came up to the well he could have looked directly at her and said, "I know exactly who you are and I know what you've done. I know that you've been married five times and that you've given up on the hope of ever having a marriage. So the man you are currently living with

is not your husband; you've decided that it's easier just to live together."
But that is not how Jesus begins. He doesn't come down on her, shame
her or destroy her dignity. Instead he simply asks, "Will you give me a
drink of water?" And everything that eventually came about through this
conversation flowed out of Jesus' initial acknowledgment of his real need
for a person who his society said had nothing of value to offer.

When we well-meaning Christians try to share Christ with others, we
tend to approach them from a place of inherent superiority. We say things
like "Hey, do you go to church?" or "Have you heard of the Four Spiritual
Laws?" or "If you were to die tonight are you sure that you would wake
up in heaven?" Usually when we ask such questions we already assume
that we know the answer. We assume that they *don't* go to church and *ha-*
ven't heard of the Four Spiritual Laws—that's why we asked. Our questions are intended to evoke a sense of need or to challenge their sense of
adequacy. This immediately puts us in the "one-up" position. So now
we're the holy one and the poor person that we're trying to evangelize is
clueless and is in need of our help.

No doubt we are really trying to be helpful when we take this approach,
but it has the adverse effect of shaming and humiliating the person. Most
people whose lives are messed up already know that they are. That's the
old story and they know it by heart. Like my friend Sam, they need a new
story and a fresh approach. They need to be affirmed as a person of worth
and value, someone who has something good to offer. We all need to be
needed. I'm not talking about a "gospel" of increased self-esteem but about
God's understanding our human need for purpose and significance.

What is the motivation for our evangelism? Maybe you're like me and
have mixed motives for sharing your faith with others. When I was
younger I used to be motivated by a sense of guilt or Christian duty. I was
concerned about what other people thought of me, and I wanted to meet
their expectations for what a good Christian person was supposed to do.
I also have to admit that it made me feel good about myself—as if every
time I won a convert to Christ carved another notch on my spirituality

belt. I felt proud of my boldness to be a witness who was not ashamed of my Christian faith. It made me feel as if I was really serious and radical for Christ.

A minister I heard in a radio interview confessed that he felt responsible for making sure that he told as many people as possible about Jesus because he could be their last chance to hear the gospel. I identified with that motivation too. We never know what the future holds for anyone, and so out of a sincere desire to make sure that my friends and family would have eternal life when they died, I would make it my personal responsibility to talk to them about Jesus.

Though these methods and motives are not bad and many people, including myself, have—and will continue to—come to faith as a result of them, I believe that Jesus gives us a new, more effective approach that challenges and expands our old notions of evangelism. It never occurred to me that evangelism and reconciliation could actually be based on our real need for people and what they have to offer.

NICE BUT NOT NECESSARY

In my travels to speak at churches, in conferences and on college campuses, I am often asked how Christian institutions and organizations can recruit and retain more women or people of color. The question usually is something like "How can we get more [you fill in the blank—women, ethnic minorities, black men, internationals, young people] to join our group, attend our church or work in our company?"

I normally answer the question with a question. I ask, "Why do you need them? Why do you need these people in your group, church or organization? How would it make your group better to have them there?" Unfortunately, most people don't have an answer for this. They're not sure. They haven't thought about it before or seriously grappled with why they need people who are different from them in their group. They haven't identified their thirst. Maybe it would be "right" or because it would be "nice" to have more diverse representation—but it is not quite *necessary*.

Far too often in my experience we Christians feel a sense of obligation about diversity. It's almost as if we feel that we "ought" to have people of different nationalities and perspectives around us to prove that we are open-minded, sincere, progressive and multicultural people. So we set about the task of getting different people to add to our numbers. This might include making sure that more women are represented, that there is a hearing-impaired ministry in our church or people of color on our staff. However, most people can tell when they are really necessary and when they are not. They know when they are just there to fill a quota system or to serve as a type of window dressing. They know that when they are *needed*, they have the ability to change and influence the organization; when it is just nice to have them around, they know this too because nothing is going to change as a result of their presence.

If the one white family or the only Latino couple in an all-black church left and that church is able to continue on exactly as it had before, it confirms that that person or family was nice but not really necessary. When a person or group is really needed, structures, policies and practices are developed to take account of their worldview, expertise, needs and experience. If we are to be credible witnesses of the gospel, we must understand that it's not *nice* for us to engage people across racial, ethnic, gender, sociopolitical and cultural lines—it's *necessary!*

Coming up against a requirement to conform to the status quo and assimilate—that is, being expected to give up their own identity to fit into the group's dominant culture—is the primary way that most people know when they are not *necessary* to an organization. In 1985 I attended a conference on gender equality from a biblical perspective in northern California. An African American woman named Michelle Borba was among the speakers; I have not seen her since that conference, but I will never forget what she said. In a powerful presentation about gender equality in the church, she said that the unspoken rule of most white evangelical organizations is "We are open to including you, but we cannot tolerate you the way you are."

When people find that they don't change or influence the cultural context but instead the context changes them, they realize that they are not really needed. When a real need for people who are different from us does not exist, our interactions with them express only our special interests or curiosity. Our cultural blinders and intercultural ignorance are revealed in stereotypical and hurtful questions and comments like those I heard quoted by students of color at a Christian college I visited. They said that well-meaning Christians asked an African American woman who is quite articulate, "Can you talk black if you really want to?" or "Is that really your hair?" A student from Guatemala was asked, "Do they drive cars in your country?" An Asian American woman was asked, "Can you see through your eyes?" These are not questions whose answers people really need to know. They are curiosity questions that will not change anything about the person asking them or about the organization they represent. In most cases, how a black woman styles her hair is not going to change how other people style theirs.

Most of the international students and people of color I meet in white evangelical institutions graciously answer these painful questions because they don't want to appear thin skinned. They also try to be patient because they understand the ignorance from which these questions arise. However, it is important that we know the difference between *nice* and *necessary* if we are going to gain credibility to share the gospel cross-culturally.

RELINQUISHING POWER

In order to acknowledge our real need for other people and to receive their unique perspectives and expertise, we will need to relinquish the power and control that keep us from being changed or influenced by them. This is not an easy thing to do. It will require an honest assessment of the power we possess—both individually and corporately—and gaining a deeper understanding of how we use it to control others in our organizations.

First we must define power and understand what it is. According to *Webster's Dictionary*, power is "the ability to do, act, produce, or affect strongly; the ability to control others; to have authority, sway or influence; a special authority assigned to or exercised by a person or a group; a nation, especially one having influence or domination over other nations." This is consistent with the definition proposed by Rev. Dr. Martin Luther King Jr.: "power is the ability to achieve purpose and effect change."

Based upon these definitions, it seems that power is the ability to make a decision, to have options, and to exercise choice and influence. Power can therefore take many different forms—political power, intellectual power (knowledge is power), economic/financial power, physical power, social power, organizational or institutional power, political power, spiritual power, technological power, decision-making power, sexual power, relational power, military power, legal power, historical power, diplomatic power. All of these can be used to bring positive change and can serve the common good, but they can also be used to manipulate and control persons and situations.

When Jesus comes to the conversation with the woman at the well, the power is stacked high on his side. He is Jewish and male. As such, he represents the dominant culture of his day and has access to the rights and privileges that are afforded to people in that leading group. He also has religious authority as a rabbi. He is well educated and has a certain amount of affluence and influence in society by virtue of his knowledge. He has relational and spiritual authority, which is evidenced by the large numbers of people who follow him and his disciples, who have left everything to accompany him. He has developed notoriety because of the preaching, teaching and healing ministry that has had an impact on multitudes of people. And even though the woman has yet to discover it, he is also the Son of God—arguably the epitome of power itself! All these things could create distance between him and the woman at the well.

My friend Sam is a Samaritan and a woman. She is from an ethnic group that is seen as inferior. She is probably not well educated, not wealthy nor from a highly respected social class. She has been married five times and is probably seen as a person of low moral standing and questionable spiritual character. This is an important point to explore in more detail before we move on too quickly, because *women could not divorce men* in that culture. Instead, it was men who divorced and rejected their wives. The grounds for divorce could range from having a physical abnormality that went undetected until after marriage to being unable to conceive and bear children. If a woman could not cook, that could be acceptable grounds for divorce! The process necessary to divorce one's wife was simply to bring her into a public place and to say three times, "I divorce you, I divorce you, I divorce you." In Sam's case, then, on five different occasions a man has told her that she is damaged goods and he doesn't want her anymore. Maybe that is why she has chosen to live with someone this time instead of getting married. Maybe she doesn't believe that anyone will love her enough to marry her again.

The Samaritan woman comes to this conversation with Jesus with very little power on her side except the right to refuse. When Jesus asks her, "Will you give me a drink?" all she knows is that he is a thirsty man, the well is deep, he doesn't have a bucket and he needs her help. By making one simple request, "Give me a drink," Jesus changes the power dynamic between the two of them. In that instant he skillfully and profoundly empowers her to be the "helper" and he becomes the "helped." Jesus has challenged the structural and personal alienation generated by their power differential. On the surface this may seem like a simple gesture, but upon closer inspection it becomes apparent that what Jesus has done is actually transformational!

What Jesus demonstrates is radically different from and even contrary to what many of us have been taught about evangelism. We have been taught to help or to serve, so the question we usually ask is "What can I or we do to help?" This is asked out of genuine care and concern, I'm sure. However, whenever we identify ourselves as the "helper," we have just taken the place of power in the relationship. Although "How can I help?" appears to be an innocent and humble question, it presupposes the power of the person or group who is asking it.

I realized this as I observed my daughter, Mia, who is the youngest person in our family. When she was just a little girl, she would ask if she could help me in the kitchen. I think on some level—unconscious perhaps even to her—she recognized that there is something very powerful about being able to help. She wanted to feel useful and important, so she would volunteer her services. Usually when she "helped" tasks took longer than they normally would. However, her ability to help empowered her: she was contributing to something important and she felt needed.

Being in a position to help others implies the inherent power to do so. When Jesus asks the Samaritan woman for her help, he gives us a different strategy of evangelism and reconciliation. Instead of offering his help first and thus establishing his place of power, Jesus limits his powerful status as a Jewish, male, well-educated rabbi and allows this woman to be his helper. In so doing he empowers her.

The implications of this could be staggering for Christian organizations and institutions as they try to find innovative ways to reach an expanding audience in a global world. The issue of power could be the ultimate reason that so many people find true reconciliation so difficult to achieve and may explain why they resist our attempts to evangelize them. It may be that they have not experienced enough people who are willing to relinquish power and be the "helped."

Most of us assume that we have the things that other people need. But this assumption hinders our ability to build bridges and win credibility in order to effectively communicate the gospel message. We unwittingly represent and wield power that asserts our dominance and control in crosscultural and international situations. Generally we have the power in our churches, institutions and organizations. We're in control, and if other people are going to partner with us they understand that they will be able to do so only on our terms.

In Christian organizations we often use language like *family* and *community* to describe our close-knit relationships. However, these terms are also used to promote a culture of sameness in which a person must assimilate to belong. When a person differs or disagrees, they can be seen as a threat to the system. Then they are isolated, cut off from the relational networks and feel ostracized from the rest of the "family." Their punishment is that they miss out on a lot of the good stuff that the group has to offer like promotions, job security, fiscal responsibility and access to information and are kept away from the power base of the organization. This creates a power distance, and the unspoken goal becomes to get them to join or assimilate but not to contribute.

If our organization is to be a credible witness of the gospel, it is critical that we recognize these power dynamics and the ways we control others. People who have not had power in the system must be empowered to give their perspectives, raise their concerns, contribute their expertise and be able to influence change. An example of a real power exchange in a Christian institution would be to authorize others to help shape the curriculum and its direction so that future generations would have access. In a U.S. church or Christian organization, it might be to allow and encourage a person to preach or teach in their native language and, if this is not English, to translate it for the listening audience to understand. The worship experience would reflect the ethnic and cultural styles of all the people involved. No one ethnicity, language or approach would control or dominate the worship experience or social climate of the group. Cultural practices regarding time, cleanliness, emotional expressiveness or the use of money would not be given negative labels when they differed from our own cultural or ethnic preferences. Contributions would come from the gifts of the Spirit, not status, education and wealth.

Such a transformation would generate what some scholars call a "hybrid culture." "This hybrid culture has the effect of shifting traditional power relationships away from those who would dominate through a familiarity with 'the system' to a more equalizing practice in which no one ethnic/racial group can claim absolute superiority." It would be like the early believers in Acts 2 who heard the gospel preached in their native languages and covenanted to meet regularly together on each other's home turf—despite their differences—to build honest and intimate relationships based on their mutual understanding of Scripture as they were guided by prayer. This informed their understanding and practice of social justice and motivated them to ensure that everyone's needs were met.

We must understand that there is something of God in every person and every culture, and in order to access it and learn from it we will have to relinquish our power and become the helped instead of always being the helper. Instead of criticizing and correcting people for doing things differently, we will ask for their help and allow them to show us new ways to experience and understand God in the world. This will mean that we will have to humble ourselves and follow their lead, even if it makes us feel uncomfortable. We will have to sing songs in languages that we don't understand or speak very well. We might have to adjust or be more flexible with our time frame for events. Our organizational structures might have to change to include different people whose voices have been marginalized because they don't have the relational or historical power to be heard within the institution.

Our Christian witness can come across very powerfully. We can use all the bells and whistles that modern technology and our money can afford to make quite an impressive and convincing presentation. However, instead of approaching people from our place of strength, Jesus is calling us to relinquish our power so that we can show the power of the gospel to bring together people from divergent backgrounds that would normally never relate to each other. To do this we must understand that we can't always be the "helper." If our message is going to have any integrity we must recognize that we also need to be helped and people who are unlike us have something valuable to give to us. Jesus relinquished his power as a member of the dominant society by asking the Samaritan woman for her help. If we are ever going to experience the Kingdom of God on earth and promote real Christianity we will have to go and do likewise.

THE POWER OF WEAKNESS

I learned this very difficult lesson at Urbana 2000, an international missions conference held at the University of Illinois in Champaign-Urbana and sponsored by InterVarsity Christian Fellowship. There would be twenty thousand delegates from all over the world at this conference, and I was invited to be one of the keynote speakers. It was a great honor to be asked, and I really wanted to preach well. In fact, if the truth were told, I wanted to knock the ball out the park! So I prepared for this speaking event as I had never prepared before. I studied. I prayed and I fasted. I wrote the sermon well ahead of time.

But in spite of all my preparation, study and prayer, I still felt like something was missing. I didn't feel *anointed*. So when my family and I went to our monthly Bible study group, I asked the group to pray for me. They all gathered around me and prayed that God would use me and anoint me to speak powerfully at Urbana. Those were the prayers I expected them to pray. However, when my husband Derek laid his hands on me to pray, he said, "Lord, Brenda represents the best of who we are. We give her to you and ask you to use her as your sacrificial lamb."

I didn't say anything, but I thought, *Sacrificial lamb! I don't want to be a sacrificial lamb! What kind of prayer is that?!* I promptly dismissed Derek's prayer and decided to side with all the people who had prayed for me to be anointed and powerfully used by God.

At Urbana I preached well, but it was not as dynamic as I had hoped. During my message I talked about Ricky Byrdsong, the former head basketball coach at Northwestern University in Evanston, Illinois, who had been tragically shot and killed by a white supremacist college student. As I told the story, I neglected to mention a young Korean graduate student who was also shot and killed in Indiana, while he was standing in front of his Presbyterian church, by the same gunman. I was afraid of mispronouncing his name in front of all those people—so I omitted it.

Later, after I finished speaking, it was brought to my attention that some Asian students were upset with me: my omission had made it seem as if I valued and mourned the life of one man more than the other. That was never what I had intended to do at Urbana!

The next morning I sensed that God spoke to me and said that I was to be a "symbol of repentance." Once again, my first response was "I don't *want* to be a symbol of repentance!" But as I discussed it with my husband, we both knew that I had to apologize. Only then did Derek's prayer about being a "sacrificial lamb" make sense to me. After much internal debate and struggle, I asked the convention leaders for time to go back onstage and apologize. They agreed and gave me two minutes.

As I spoke, I was broken and humbled. I felt weak and vulnerable in front of thousands of people. Ending my remarks, I said, "I now understand what it feels like to be white—to try so hard to get it right but feel like you always get it wrong." That was the first time that I honestly identified and empathized with white people.

There was an immediate reaction throughout the assembly hall. The worship leader standing onstage began to cry. One woman later told me that she had watched the service on closed-circuit television in her hotel room and when she heard those words she gasped and began to weep.

Many would say that that apology was a turning point at Urbana. The positive responses I received were overwhelming. As I left the stage, the next speaker, Ken Fong, hugged me and said he was proud of me. Since then we have become close colleagues in the ministry of reconciliation. International delegates from Korea bowed and greeted me with honor. Asian American, Native American and Hispanic students welcomed and greeted me warmly when I visited their ethnic-specific gatherings. I was given invitations to speak in Africa and other countries. God used that two-minute apology more powerfully than he used the entire message I preached at Urbana!

I was indeed used as God's "sacrificial lamb," and in the process I learned about the power of weakness. I learned that humility is one of the most important characteristics in the ministry of reconciliation. This is implied in the very nature of the word *humility*, which comes from the Latin word *humus* and means "fertile ground." Our humility is the fertile ground that draws the supernatural power of God to us. This power, which is revealed through our weakness, breaks down walls and unites people. Humility is the fertile ground necessary to receive the seeds of new visions, new possibilities, new strategies and new ideas that can grow into relationships and communities that reflect the kingdom of God.

REGAINING OUR EVANGELISTIC CREDIBILITY

When is the last time that you've been in a relationship with someone that society says is inferior to you? When have you put yourself in a position to be helped by someone who is different and who could honestly influence you or your organization? In order to restore our credibility to preach the gospel of Jesus Christ, we will have to recognize that there are people without a high school diploma who have something they can teach us. There is an elderly woman or deacon in the church who has the power of prayer, and when he or she lays hands on the sick they recover. There might be a stay-at-home mom or a single mother who knows more about raising children than we do, and we need their help. There might be a homeless man on the corner who knows the answer to how to help your loved one get off drugs.

If we are going to regain our evangelistic credibility, we must recognize our need for people who are different from us and invite them into our lives. We must be willing to acknowledge this and say to them, *I need you*. Instead of evangelizing from a place of power, we would begin by affirming that other people have something valuable to offer *us*. This will radically change how we approach people and how we invite them to attend our Christian functions. We might approach them by saying something like "I'm asking you to come join our church because we really need you; we're impoverished without you and the knowledge you bring." Or, "You understand and have access to a community of people who know and trust you. We need your help and guidance to establish our credibility, and we will follow your lead." Still another message might be "We need you to be on our board of directors because of your perspective and life experience. Without your thought, your insight, your point of view, we don't have everything we need to be effective. There's a piece of the puzzle that's missing without you, and we need your contribution. It's not just nice to have you; it's really necessary, and that's why we have asked you to come, speak and share your wisdom and expertise. We respect you and will demonstrate this by implementing what you recommend."

How much would our organization be improved and enriched by the presence and contributions of people who are unlike us? How would this increase our ability to witness more effectively to the reality of the gospel? When our thirst for God's kingdom grows greater, we will make the necessary adjustments to include people in our lives and in our organizations who are not presently there. Little do we know, but it is "high noon" and we are wearied from our journey. It is high time for us to recognize that we will die of thirst if we don't acknowledge our real need for others and empower them to give the water that only people different from us can bring.

5

TAKE RISKS TO REACH OUT

The Samaritan woman said to him, "How is it that you, a Jew, ask a drink of me, a woman of Samaria?" (Jews do not share things in common with Samaritans.)

JOHN 4:9

There are some conversations that you never forget. For me it was one I had with Mark and Peter, two young evangelists from Singapore, while we were all students at Fuller Theological Seminary in Pasadena, California. One day we were discussing our different philosophies and approaches to evangelism. I said it was important to me to give an altar call at the conclusion of every sermon I preached. I felt that if a person had been fully persuaded by what I said and if God was at work in their heart, they should acknowledge it by making a decision to accept Jesus in that moment. I reasoned that this would prove their sincerity and openness to the power of the Holy Spirit.

After I finished explaining my position, both men challenged me about my thinking and methods of evangelism. They said they would never expect a person to make a life-changing decision to accept and follow Jesus Christ on the same night the gospel was first preached to them. In fact, they would be suspicious of anyone who made a decision like that too hastily. It would indicate that the person had not thought carefully enough about the risks and the costliness of their decision, that they hadn't soberly considered the possible price they might have to pay, like being disowned by their family, ostracized from their community, or beaten or killed for their faith. Instead of encouraging a potential convert to come to the altar, they would counsel that person to wait and go home to really think about all the ramifications before they made a firm decision. If after an extended period of personal reflection and soul searching they still wanted to accept Jesus Christ as their Lord and Savior, they would then be invited to do so.

At first I was shocked: I had assumed that all Christians agreed with the basic premise that we get sinners to repent and accept Jesus right then and there! I had never considered the fact that people do evangelism differently in other parts of the world. As I stood there stunned, I considered the wisdom of what they had said. I realized that my approach to evangelism was culturally conditioned by a society that tends to do things quick, fast and in a hurry. I also had to admit that I didn't know anything about having to suffer, in the way they described, for the gospel. For the most part, I didn't have to worry about being persecuted for my faith in the United States. I hadn't known that when I was calling a person to Jesus I was also calling them to take risks.

RISK TAKING IN SAMARIA

I believe that the Samaritan woman knew what it was to suffer. She was discriminated against, marginalized and oppressed by the Jews because of her ethnicity and her gender. Jesus was a Jew and therefore represented the dominant culture. These were the people who used their power to institutionalize and justify their social injustice and bigoted practices against the Samaritans.

So when Sam comes to the well and saw Jesus sitting there, my guess is that she is not happy to see him! And when he goes even further to ask her for a drink of water, she greets his request with open indignation.

The Samaritan woman said to him; "How is it that you, a Jew, ask a drink of me, a woman of Samaria?" (Jews do not share things in common with Samaritans.) (John 4:9)

She hasn't gone to the well to have a social interaction—and she definitely didn't expect to have one with a Jewish man!

Jesus took a risk to go through Samaria, and he took an even greater risk to ask for water from a woman who has been discriminated against and hurt by his people. It was like adding insult to injury for him to want something from her. It's one thing to be in someone else's neighborhood as a tourist, but it's another thing altogether to be there as an outsider who wants something from that community. It is a risk to acknowledge our need, because some people may misinterpret our request and see our presence as a threat to their community. When Jesus asked my friend Sam for a drink of water, she could have remembered all of the hurt she had endured from the Jews and could have put her hand on her hip and said in no uncertain terms, "How dare you come into my community and ask for something! You Jews think you own everything and everybody! I'm tired of the way you treat my people. I'm tried of the way you think you can boss us around, as if we were your slaves! You will die of thirst before I give you something to drink! You may control things in Jerusalem, but you don't control things in my neighborhood!"

HURT PEOPLE HURT PEOPLE

To understand her mistrustful response, it's important to remember that my friend Sam has been ostracized and criticized. She has been ridiculed, talked about and humiliated—not just by the Jews but also by people of her own ethnic group. No doubt her self-esteem was in the toilet and she didn't feel like socializing with anybody that day—and certainly not a

Jew! Likely her hurt and shame had become toxic and spilled over into most of her social situations and personal relationships. This is what happens when people have been deeply hurt.

The dynamics of this is discussed in a book that is simply yet profoundly titled *Hurt People Hurt People,* by Sandra Wilson and Ronald Eggert. The authors suggest that when people have been hurt by life circumstances or the mistreatment of others, they have the tendency to take it out on the people close to them or those with whom they interact. It may not be intentional, but they hurt other people as a result of the personal wounds and emotional scars that they carry.

This dynamic seems to be especially at work when we are trying to bridge the gaps between people of different ethnic groups, nationalities, social classes or genders. The historic hurts and injustices that people have endured, and continue to endure, can cause them to hurt unsuspecting people who had nothing to do with the original offense. Although a person who is new to the situation may have sincere motives and intentions, they are viewed with suspicion and disdain because they represent the people group that has done hurtful things in the past. The hurt and anger that is unleashed may not be meant to be a personal attack. It is the rage of people who have been hurt by political, social and economic structures or who have experienced personal tragedy and now feel justified in protecting themselves from more pain.

When we try to engage people with the gospel, they may question our motives because Christians have hurt them or they have been mistreated by people of our ethnic group. They may not be happy to see us coming and may not greet us with an enthusiastic response. They may view us as a part of the problem and not as a part of the solution.

I learned this in a painful way during a trip to England with a team of African American seminarians from Fuller Theological Seminary. One of the last places we visited was an impoverished community in Birmingham, where many Jamaican people lived. I expected this to be one of our best visits because we were going to be with people who looked like us.

Instead, when we arrived we were met with anger and hostility. One young woman, Mavis, acted as the spokesperson for the group, and she said with vehemence in her voice, "Where have you been? Didn't you know about the suffering we were experiencing here in England?" She went on to explain to us that there had been riots in Birmingham in protest of the poor living conditions and lack of opportunity that faced most black British. We learned that many Jamaicans had moved to England after World War II to help rebuild the country. They hoped to make a better life for themselves and to finally be accepted as full-fledged British citizens. However, after decades of service they were no longer needed, and they were relegated to a lower-class existence with no hope of ever being accepted as fully British. This frustration built up and finally spilled over in social unrest because the subsequent generations of Jamaican people born in England felt like foreigners in the land of their birth. They did not have a home anywhere. They were now considered foreigners in Jamaica, and they were never going to be given full and equal status in Britain.

As those of us from the United States listened to this story, we were totally dumbfounded and caught off guard. The black British were angry because of our lack of involvement and our seeming indifference. Our silence had bred consent, and we were complicit in an unjust and corrupt system that was destroying the life chances of people who looked just like us. Our only response was to apologize and to confess that we really hadn't known. We hadn't known that there were people waiting for us, who needed us to come and share what we had learned through our struggle as people of African descent in America.

The black British did not rise up and call us blessed. Similarly, there will be days when people will unleash their anger and hurt on you as a means to express their outrage at an unjust system. This is the risk we take as we heed the call to embrace real Christianity. It's not always going to be nice and neat. In fact, at times it will be messy. People will wonder what you're doing in their community, why you've joined their church, what's your ulterior motive. They will view you with suspicion and wonder when you are going to get tired of visiting and leave. They will think, *What does he or she really want?* In your heart you will know that you're just living out the gospel and trying to be the kingdom representative that God has called you to be.

This is the risk we take. We may not be well received. There are no guarantees.

RISKY BUSINESS

It is risky business to pursue the kingdom of God. I wish I could tell you that everybody you meet in your "Samaria" will be happy to see you. I wish I could tell you that they're going to kiss you and smile and be so glad that you came. I wish I could say that nobody is going to curse you out when you go to Samaria. But the truth is, sometimes we will be called everything but a child of God.

I can't promise that it will be safe and comfortable when we try to cross racial, cultural, gender, religious, political or generational divides. Those of us who want to be a credible witness must be willing to take risks. In fact, I have found that individuals, groups or leaders in organizations who are highly risk-aversive will paralyze the reconciliation process and inadvertently lead others to doubt if a kingdom vision is actually possible. Churches and Christian groups then become unable to trust God for innovative and new ways to do cutting-edge ministry that will really engage the culture around them. The consequence of this is the loss of life and vitality that results when we choose to play it safe. This seems to be implied in what Jesus said to his followers in Matthew 10:39: we must be willing to lose our lives to find them. When we follow Jesus and seek to demonstrate the truth and power of the gospel, we are taking a risk. It is a risk to go where others dare not go. It's a risk to do more than talk about Jesus. Talking about Jesus is one thing; really following him in our choices about relationships, where we purchase property, how we vote and spend our money—that's another! Our attempts to follow might cause us to lose relationships with those that we love, to lose donors who had given us financial support, or to lose our prestige or reputation in certain social circles. This may be the risk we have to take in order to be a credible witness.

When I moved to Chicago from Pasadena, several people took me under their wing and helped me to get acclimated to life and ministry in the city. One such person was Pastor Wayne Gordon at Lawndale Community Christian Church. Lawndale is an inner-city community on the west side of Chicago that has been characterized by poverty, crime and the failure of its local school system. However, Gordon, who is affectionately called Coach because he started his ministry with teenagers through sports, has led Lawndale Community Church to become a premier congregation specializing in Christian community development, and the neighborhood is being transformed and revitalized.

One day, having spent a few hours visiting with Coach at the church, I returned to my car to discover that all four of my hubcaps had been stolen. I was angry and hurt. I thought to myself, *This is not right! This is not fair! I'm a black woman. I'm one of the "good guys." Didn't these people know that I'm a sister?* I didn't have a lot of money. I wasn't a part of the unjust system. They weren't supposed to steal my hubcaps!

When I went back into the church to tell Coach what happened, he didn't bat an eye or get upset at all. He simply looked at me and said something like "That's a reality of living and working in the city. What makes you think that you'd be exempt from what everyone else has to face?" I know now that sin does not discriminate and that the fact that we love Jesus doesn't mean that bad things can't happen to us. That's the risk we take—just ask my friend Coach.

THE RISK OF TRUST

Although Jesus intentionally went into a community where he risked being viewed with suspicion and treated with contempt, it is also true that the Samaritan woman took a risk to interact with a person from a different ethnic group, social class and religion from her own. She made it quite clear that she knew that they should not have any dealings with each other. She may have risked being further ostracized for being disloyal to her community by "fraternizing with the enemy." Her standing with her own people could have been further diminished because she chose to interact with Jesus. Perhaps she risked being viewed as a "cheap woman" who was coming on to a strange man in public for sexual gratification or financial gain. Her reputation was already questionable, and she certainly didn't need any more rumors to further diminish it.

So I think my friend Sam is taking a risk to have this conversation with Jesus. Furthermore, as their conversation continues, she is asked to take one of the biggest risks of all—to reconsider what she has been taught about religion and pursue a real, personal relationship with God. This is not an easy thing to do, especially if the challenge is coming from a person we're not sure we can trust.

When I tried to be a spiritual leader to a young Asian American woman who proved to be afraid of African American people, I became aware of how an inability to trust can seriously hinder our ability to do ministry. At first I was deeply offended and took her withdrawal and seeming fear of me very personally. I decided that she was racist and questioned whether she should stay in the program I was leading. However, one day during a small group session, she told her story and explained why she was afraid of black people. Her mother and father had owned a grocery store in an inner-city neighborhood. During an attempted robbery her mother was shot and killed. The man who committed this horrible crime was African American, and since then she had been deathly afraid of African American people—including me.

I looked like a person who caused her immeasurable pain and suffering. It might take years for her to trust that all African Americans are not threatening in some way. I understood this and thereafter tried to demonstrate the love of Jesus; however, we never quite made a connection. She was afraid of me, recoiled when I touched her and had difficulty following my leadership. I continued to serve her but was limited in my ability to influence her with the gospel, because that was dependent on whether she would take the risk to trust.

In the same way, the Samaritan woman must take the risk of engaging with a man who looks like the dominant culture that has hurt and oppressed her. When a person has suffered pain or injustice, they don't easily trust people who represent or remind them of the offense. Further, people who have been marginalized by society are naturally skeptical and fearful of strangers who come into their community in need of assistance or offering to help. It could be that they have been used by politicians who come when they need votes but then never keep their promises. Then there have been the census takers who come in a community because they need information, but the data collected is later used to displace the people who divulged it. For these reasons and more, if we want to want to effectively share the gospel it is critical that we establish ourselves as credible witnesses *who can be trusted.*

One way for us to do this is to come into new situations as inductive learners. That means that we may have to put away our preconceived notions, our ready-made answers and solutions. Instead our posture is to seek more to understand than to be understood. To do this we will need to ask more questions, listen more carefully and learn about life from another person's point of view. However, let me hasten to say that we do well to avoid the interrogation type of inquiries that arouse more fear—like those of census takers. In crosscultural situations, well-meaning people who are trying to get to know me as an African American woman often ask me probing questions in rapid-fire succession: "What do you do? Where do you live? What does your husband do? How long have you lived there? How many children do you have? Where do they go to school?" Now I know that these questions are asked in a sincere attempt to get to know me, but when a person has been reared in a community where such questions are received with justified suspicion because of immigration issues or the fear of social stigma, being bombarded with them can feel threatening. As an alternative, I would suggest that we must first express our need for the other person and thereby take the risk to make ourselves vulnerable.

These are just some of the risks that we might need to take to be a credible witness of the gospel. If you are a member of the dominant culture, you may be seen as a symbol of the group that has often hurt, oppressed and dominated others. In the same way, those in our society and around the world may mistrust us as Christians because the church is sometimes identified with political and social power. Still, we must take the risk of exposing our faith and ourselves to those who may see life very differently. This may mean that we risk experiencing rejection, anger, hostility or ridicule as people unfairly question our integrity and misinterpret our motives. Or if we are like my friend Sam, we will need to take the risk of trusting that there is a new way to look at Scripture and understand the gospel that we have not considered. Being open to reexamine and rethink what we have been taught about God and believed all our lives is not an easy thing to do. It's a risk.

I am often helped and encouraged by the words I heard Cornel West, the distinguished theologian and scholar, say at the conclusion of a lecture he gave at the University of Chicago: "My brothers and my sisters, I am no longer optimistic, because optimism implies having hope in what we see. What I am asking us to do is to take a massive leap of *faith!*" Dr. West is right: this is the risk the world needs more and more of us to take.

6

DEVELOP RECIPROCITY
AND INTERDEPENDENCE

*Jesus answered her, "If you knew the gift of God, and who it is
that is saying to you, 'Give me a drink,' you would have asked
him, and he would have given you living water."*

JOHN 4:10

One day when my son, Omari, was in the fourth grade, his teacher
asked if I could teach a session for her class on diversity and reconciliation. She wanted her children to learn how to get along with and embrace
human differences. She said that my son had proudly mentioned that I
provide ethnic diversity training on college and university campuses, and
she wondered if I could do a short version for fourth graders.

I'm not sure why—perhaps I was caught up in the joy of learning that
my son talked about me at school and was proud of what I do—but I
agreed. As the day for my presentation grew closer, though, I got nervous
and doubted my ability to help fourth-grade students understand such
complex issues as ethnocentrism, racism and reconciliation. How could I

make such a difficult topic accessible to children? In my desperation I grabbed one of my children's puzzles and took it to school on the morning of the presentation. I hoped to use the puzzle as a metaphor for diversity that might be fun and engaging for the kids. If all else failed, at least they would have a good time because my son had already warned me that I couldn't embarrass him by messing up!

When I walked into the classroom, the kids were seated at their desks, eager to get started with the special presentation. After the teacher introduced me, I handed a puzzle piece to each student in the class. As I began my spiel about how diversity is like a puzzle, I noticed that the children in the back of the class were busily working on something rather than paying attention to me. They chattered with excitement as they passed objects back and forth between them.

I asked what they were doing, and they announced, "We're putting it together!" When I asked them why, they said, "It's a puzzle. The pieces are supposed to go together. It doesn't make any sense if we don't put all of our pieces together."

Standing in that classroom, I realized that these children from different backgrounds were teaching me. They didn't need instruction about the importance of coming together—they instinctively knew that our individual pieces "don't make sense" unless they come together with other pieces of different shapes, sizes and colors. They understood that they were interdependent, and they eagerly collaborated with each other so they could see the bigger picture. To do anything less just wouldn't have made sense.

RECIPROCITY AT THE WELL

Jesus models this type of interdependent relationship in our Scripture text when he asks for well water from the Samaritan woman and then offers her living water in return. The woman has been apprehensive about Jesus and reluctant to give him what he needs. Although she does not flatly deny his request, she is a bit rude when she reminds him that Jews and Samaritans do not have any friendly dealings with each other. Jesus responds, "If you knew the gift of God, and who it is that is saying to you, 'Give me a drink,' you would have asked him, and he would have given you living water" (John 4:10).

Not convinced, the woman argues that Jesus has nothing to draw water with and the well is too deep for him to produce fresh spring water without assistance. There was no permanent rope or bucket attached to the well that could be lowered to retrieve water. And since good water was not plentiful and was therefore a precious commodity, travelers had to carry leather pouches or buckets and a cord with them to get water out of deep wells. Sam observes that Jesus has nothing like this with him: "Sir, you have no bucket, and the well is deep. Where do you get that living water? Are you greater than our ancestor Jacob, who gave us the well, and with his sons and his flocks drank from it?" (John 4:11-12).

She may be assuming that Jesus was referring to some better well in that region and thereby implying that he has more knowledge or skill than Jacob. However, Jesus ignores her objections based upon ancient hostilities and boldly declares that although her observations are correct, he also has something valuable to offer. He acknowledges his need for help but doesn't apologize for being a Jew. Even though the history of bigotry, prejudice and oppression between their people is undeniable, Jesus knows that he is a gift from God who has the power to change my friend Sam's life. So instead of retreating and in spite of his apparent limitations, he asserts confidently that he also has a significant gift to contribute to the relationship.

This is an important lesson for us to learn that can empower and embolden our evangelism. Every person, every culture, every ethnic group and every nationality has a unique piece of the puzzle that reflects the image of God. We do not serve the "greater good" or advance the kingdom when we become paralyzed in self-loathing and navel gazing about our shortcomings or those of our people group.

I have met many people who are brokenhearted about the state of current affairs in America and around the world. They are pained about the wars and the violence that are destroying so many innocent people. They lament the racial tensions and ethnic strife that are devastating many parts of our country and many regions of the world. Wishing to identify with those who are suffering and to distance themselves from perpetrators of injustice, they express regret about being from a certain ethnic group or nationality. In crosscultural conversations they may say things like "I'm so sorry that I'm white" or "I'm ashamed to be an American." It is as if they wished they were born into another ethnicity or nationality. They want to be forgiven for being a part of their particular group and are apologetic about where they live and the privileges they may have.

It would be wrong to ignore the injustices suffered by others and focus on just enjoying one's privileges. But it is also wrong to waste precious time begging to be forgiven and apologizing for things over which we have no control while there are people who need what we have to offer and there is important work to be done. Beating ourselves up for our own identity and culture is not helpful in restoring our Christian credibility. Instead, we need to know ourselves, to be who we are and to recognize that we have something unique to offer others. It takes courage and humility to look reality in the face and honestly say, "My people or my country have done many things that were wrong and I acknowledge them as sin. However, I am going to use my life to get involved and address as many of these injustices as I can." This is how we demonstrate our credibility—not by sitting on the sidelines but by getting in the game!

GLOBAL INTERDEPENDENCE

The challenge of understanding and embracing our mutual interdependence was made powerfully clear to me by Pastor Oscar Muriu of Nairobi Chapel in Kenya, who spoke at the 2006 Urbana Missions Convention in St. Louis. I listened with over twenty-two thousand other delegates as he gave a compelling keynote address in which he declared that there is an evangelistic explosion happening in Africa, Asia and South America. Using the African church as an example, he noted, "At the beginning of the twentieth century it was estimated that the African church had 9 million converts, but by the end of that same century the church had grown to an amazing 360 million converts!" This has huge ramifications for the future of our evangelistic efforts: as a result of this astounding growth, more than 75 percent of all Protestant Christians now live in the non-Western Two-Thirds World.

These changes, said Pastor Muriu, demand a greater interdependence among all Christians around the world. He dramatized the point by paraphrasing the words of 1 Corinthians 12:14-17, where the apostle Paul uses the analogy of the human body to encourage interdependence and mutual respect among all believers within the church. Pastor Muriu called for an interdependent global church:

If the American church should say that because I am not African I do not belong to the body, it would not for that reason cease to be part of the body. If the Canadian church should say that because I am not Asian I do not belong to the body, it would not for that reason cease to be part of the body. If the whole body were European, where would the sense of joy be? And if the whole body were African, where would the sense of order be? But in fact, God has arranged the parts of the body, every one of them, just as he wanted them to be. If they were all one part, where would the body be? As it is, there are many parts, but one body. The Canadian church cannot say to the Asian church, "I don't need you." And the American church cannot say to the African church, "I don't need you." On the contrary, the Asian parts that seem to be weaker are indispensable. And the African parts that we think are less honorable should be treated with special honor. And the Latin American parts that seem unpresentable are treated with special modesty—while the presentable parts like the big, wealthy American church need no special treatment. But God has combined the members of the body, and has given greater honor to the parts that lacked it, so that there should be no division in the body but that its parts should have equal concern for each other. If one part suffers, every part suffers with it. If one part is honored, every part rejoices with it. Now you are the body of Christ, and each one of you is a part of it.

A NEW PARADIGM OF PARTNERSHIP

Paul's analogy, elaborated globally by Pastor Muriu, persuasively illustrates why it is essential for us to recognize our interdependence and need for others. Many of us American Christians have to come to a much-needed awareness that we are limited in our ability to lead people to the kingdom of God by ourselves. Although our country was built on the value of "rugged individualism" and this value has influenced how we have done evangelism in the past, such an approach is no longer sufficient to keep up with the collective global community that is emerging all around us. In his book *Evangelism Outside the Box: New Ways to Help People Experience the Good News,* Rick Richardson makes a similar point about postmodern culture: "A gospel that merely addresses an individual's personal guilt and has no answer to the addictions and evil and bondage of our day will seem irrelevant and reductionistic. In the end such a gospel will not be taken seriously in our postmodern world."

Pastor Muriu is right in calling us to recognize that the image of God has been invested in every culture and people group. Historically, the actions of U.S. Christians suggest that we have not believed this. We have not recognized our need for others, which may be why we have stayed ethnically and racially segregated in the church, in our local communities and on our college and university campuses. We have assumed that we didn't need to learn from or partner with people who are ethnically different from us. Rarely have I seen American university students seek out international students on their campus and ask their perspective or consult with them. We tend to see ourselves as self-sufficient and somewhat superior to others.

The new global realities and demographic shifts that we face might be the wake-up call we've needed to help us realize that we must partner with other people because they have a worldview that we need to thrive as the church. Partnership will require that we learn how to collaborate well with others, so we may need to understand more about different cultures and learn to speak more than one language. In my experience, people from other countries around the world speak multiple languages—fluently! This suggests that they recognize their need for others and are therefore students of the world.

As we allow our evangelistic efforts to be transformed by interdependence, I hope that we will discover that what Dr. Martin Luther King Jr. said continues to be true: "We are all caught in an inescapable network of mutuality, tied into a single garment of destiny. Whatever affects one directly, affects all indirectly." What affects people in Japan does affect me. The devaluing of the peso in Mexico has implications for our economy in the United States. The suffering of children orphaned by the AIDS pandemic in Africa has implications for the future stability of the United States. We are a part of an interdependent global community—whether we like it or not—and if we are going to seize this strategic moment in history to be a credible witness of the gospel, it will need to be in partnership with people who don't look like us. These partnerships must be reciprocal and mutually beneficial to be life giving and to advance God's kingdom on earth.

Our evangelism and reconciliation efforts must affirm and demonstrate the truth that every person, every culture and every nation has something valuable to offer and contribute to the world. It is in the splendor and beauty of our own cultures and nationalities that we embrace a new paradigm of evangelism that brings all the pieces of the puzzle together—and we understand that to do anything less just doesn't make sense.

GO BEYOND THE SUPERFICIAL

Jesus said to her, "Everyone who drinks of this water will be thirsty again, but those who drink of the water that I will give them will never be thirsty. The water that I will give will become in them a spring of water gushing up to eternal life."

JOHN 4:13-14

For years I masqueraded as a Christian. Like many young people, I knew how to go through all the right motions and emotions, but I didn't have a mature devotion. I was appropriately repentant for my sins when I needed to be. I respected my elders and made sure that I curtailed any sinful activities until I was far away from their watchful eyes. On occasion I even "got happy" and danced in the Spirit with tears streaming down my face because I felt so moved. I was simply a "churchy" girl. I sang in the choir, attended church and Sunday school regularly, sat up in front and paid attention to the sermon, and helped in any way that I could. In my own estimation I was a "good girl," and few people would have questioned my depth or sincerity.

However, when I graduated from high school and went away to college, that facade began to crumble. I met new friends who were much more worldly wise than I was. I was a good dancer, and one of the ways that I found to be accepted—and respected—by this new crowd of friends was to go to lots of parties. Unfortunately, I partied several nights a week, to the detriment of my academic studies. I also started smoking cigarettes and marijuana as a part of my new hip persona. I began to date college guys who seemed much more mature than the boyfriends that I had in high school. I was slowly creating a lifestyle that was dangerously self-destructive and completely devoid of any real meaning and purpose.

I had a number of close calls that should have driven this point home to me, but my desire to fit in was stronger than my churchy persona. One such time was when I attended a party near New York City in an upscale apartment complex. I went with my then boyfriend, whom I trusted to keep me safe. I had no idea at the time how naive, unsophisticated and insecure I really was. I didn't know that beneath my facade of being the life of the party was an insecure little girl who was desperately looking for love and acceptance. I was thrilled that I was at such a chic party with so many impressive people. However, the night turned sour for me when the host of the party came behind the sofa where I was sitting, put his hand under my chin, lifted my head up and, without asking my permission, put an inhaler under my nose. It contained some type of drug that instantly caused me to get high.

I was disoriented, scared, angry and devastated. I jumped to my feet and told him never to do that again, using every expletive I could think of! He only smiled and calmly said, "Oh baby, I wouldn't hurt you. I just didn't want to blow your high."

As I calmed down and collected myself, I thought, *What else will people do without asking my permission because they just want to see my reaction? What else would someone do to feed their own desires and hungers? What am I doing here?* That night I realized that I was trying to be a good girl in the fast lane and that people out here didn't play by my rules. Like my friend Sam, I sensed my thirst for something more in my life—something that, although I had tried, I apparently couldn't provide for myself.

A DEEPER THIRST

Most students of the Bible believe that the Samaritan woman came to the well as an outsider within her own culture. Like Jesus, she was a tired, thirsty traveler, but her journey was on the road of life. She brought her jar to the well because she needed water, but her thirst was deeper than she could supply.

When Jesus asked her for a drink, she responded sarcastically and sharply, with a mix of anger, disorientation and shame. She didn't seem to want to be bothered with small talk or polite conversation. She'd been through too much for that. When life has beaten you, there can be a crude honesty that sets aside social niceties.

Jesus could have been put off by her seemingly rude reaction, but instead he responded in a way that has the potential to change how we approach people who are seeking out of a deeper thirst. He resisted the distractions of her social, cultural and religious objections. In fact, he seemed to totally ignore them! Instead he simply, yet firmly, offered her something that was almost too good to be true. He gave Sam the opportunity to try something that was interesting, intriguing and inviting—and the offer made her want to know more.

Jesus said to the woman, "If you knew the gift of God, and who it is that is saying to you, 'Give me a drink,' you would have asked him, and he would have given you *living water.*" Jesus used this term—commonly used by people who lived in that region to mean spring water as opposed to stagnant water—to arouse her curiosity. Her physical thirst became a metaphor leading into a deeper conversation that would push her to realize that she was really thirsty for something beyond the obvious.

Her interest was captured and she was drawn to know more: Living water? Where do you get that from? Jesus' recognition of her unspoken need captured this woman's attention and drew her into an encounter that ultimately changed her life.

The Bible offers us a number of examples of Christ responding to human needs. He heals, feeds and opens eyes all as external signs of spiritual activity. Our own efforts to bring people to faith in Jesus must not ignore their difficult circumstances and physical needs. This means we must engage them with a spiritual ear for the deeper thirst and an understanding of the context of their well. Rather than telling non-Christians what to do or participating in theological, social or political debates, how about offering them something so intriguing that they will want to know more and begin to ask questions?

This would require us to know enough of their culture, social conditions and religious ideas to get beyond some superficial conversations. This insight will enable us not to be distracted but to be knowledgeable about their terrain. Of course we'll have to move beyond clichés like "Do you know Jesus? You ought to come to church" or "You need to get your life together." Instead we would want to say things like Jesus said to my friend Sam—things that come out of our recognition of a person's deeper need and that would make them pause and ask questions. Jesus is intriguing and engaging, and our efforts to introduce people to him and his kingdom should reflect that. As his witnesses we must make every effort to present him in ways that will cause people to want to find out about him and investigate his claims.

EXCHANGING THE COUNTERFEIT FOR THE REAL THING

When Jesus said that he had access to "living water" that would so completely satisfy my friend Sam's thirst that she would never get thirsty again or have to return to the well, she was totally engaged. She asked him to give her this living water. But instead of granting her request, he responded, "Go, call your husband, and come back."

Why not simply give her what she has asked for? Jesus knew that she was a tired, thirsty woman who was in need of a more satisfying life. Why not meet her obvious need for renewal right then and there? Why does she have to go and get her husband?

Jesus seems to want something more than a quid pro quo exchange. I'm not sure what the woman thought about Jesus' strange request. She may have wondered what her husband had to do with water. In any case, she responded to his directive evasively and did not go into any real detail about her marital situation. Likely she lacked the emotional energy to explain all the drama that had occurred in her life. So she simply said, "I have no husband." She saw no need to get into the sordid details. In essence her answer seems to be, "Suffice it to say, I'm not married."

To this Jesus responded with prophetic precision: "You are right in saying, 'I have no husband'; for you have had five husbands, and the one you have now is not your husband."

This is an important place to pause and talk about the insatiable nature of sin. I don't believe that the Samaritan woman just woke up one day and decided to get married five different times. My guess is that each time she met a man and married she hoped that it would last. Unfortunately, however, the truth is that in our human, sinful nature our best efforts are always and only temporary. Sure, the method that we use to try to fill the hole in our soul will feel good for a while, be it marriage, money or something else. People who say that being a non-Christian is a terrible life are not being completely honest. It takes a while before you get to the bad part. However, it is equally true that nothing else we try will ever completely satisfy our deepest thirst for a life that has meaning and purpose. Like my friend Sam, we will discover that what Jesus said in John 4:13-14 is true: "Everyone who drinks of this water will be thirsty again, but those who drink of the water that I will give them will never be thirsty. The water that I will give will become in them a spring of water gushing up to eternal life."

I have learned that no matter what we choose instead of Jesus Christ, we will always have to keep going back to that same "well" over and over to get more "water." It just doesn't last. I think that is why Jesus instructed the Samaritan woman to go get her husband and come back: he wanted her to clearly identify the "well" that she was using to try and quench her emotional and spiritual thirst. He was saying that before he could give her the real thing, she needed to acknowledge and carefully consider the counterfeit she has been using. He told her to go get her husband because being with men is the way that she had been trying to quench her thirst for many years.

Take a moment and think about what would Jesus tell you to get and bring back. I don't know what you've been using to quench your thirst. I don't know what "wells" you keep returning to over and over again, but I do know that Jesus is absolutely right when he says, "Everyone who drinks this water will get thirsty again and again." It will always be temporary, and it will never completely satisfy. I didn't think that smoking, partying and getting high on occasion would become part of my *lifestyle*. They were just things I did recreationally to be cool and fit in with my friends. But I learned that sin tends to creep up and take hold of your life in very unexpected ways, because it has an insatiable appetite—it keeps demanding to be fed.

When people get into sexual relationships outside of marriage, they don't generally intend to have one affair after another or to eventually get infected with the HIV virus or AIDS. And people who are addicted to drugs or alcohol didn't make a decision to throw their lives away and become alcoholics or drug addicts. No! These were not bad people. Instead they were thirsty and were trying to find some way to quench the longing that is deep inside of every single one of us. Unfortunately they found that what Jesus said is true: everyone who who drinks this water will be thirsty again . . . and again . . . and again . . . and again. No matter what our "well" is and no matter how good it feels, the methods that we choose to try to quench our inner thirst can slowly, over time, take us far away from God, and if left unchecked, they can destroy our life.

That's why it is important for Jesus to bring the insatiable nature of sin to our attention. He caused the Samaritan woman to consider the way that she had been trying to fill the hole in her soul through romantic relationships, and she had to face the reality that it wasn't working.

How about you? What would Jesus tell you to go and bring back? Maybe you would have to go and bring back your car or your wallet with all your credit cards. Maybe you would have to go and bring back your boyfriend or your girlfriend, your children, your job or your spouse. It might be your home, your sports trophies, your diploma or the plaques and awards that adorn your walls. In essence he would be asking you to bring back those things that define you. What are you getting your sense of meaning and purpose from? What are you using to fill up the emptiness you feel? Identify it, name it and bring it to Jesus. He wants to make a deal with us, to exchange the counterfeit that we've been using for the real thing.

So let's bring it back. Can't you just imagine the piles of things we would all return with! Perhaps you've had three kids and although it's great, being a parent hasn't filled the inner void you feel: you would bring your children back and recommit them to God. Maybe you're married and that's not completely satisfying: you and your spouse would come and offer yourselves back to God. Perhaps you have climbed to the top of the corporate ladder and you make lots of money but you're still not happy. You drive a fancy car, you've got a really nice house and lots and lots of stuff, but you still feel empty inside. Maybe you would bring the things that are status symbols for you and give them back to God. Or you might often eat when you're not hungry or shop until you drop, but at the end of the day you still feel unsatisfied, and you have to keep coming to that same old "well" over and over again. Maybe you would have to bring back the clothes you never wear or the foods you binge on when you are under stress.

Jesus has something better to offer us—something that is both internal and eternal, something that we don't have to keep schlepping our bucket back to the well to get. Jesus promises that "the water I give will become in them a spring of water gushing up to eternal life." Everything my friend

Sam seems to have tried thus far has been outside herself—external re-sources. Now Jesus offers her and us access to an internal resource that will function like an underground spring that gives a constant supply of refreshment and produces spiritual life. It really is an offer too good to refuse. It is an offer to experience transformation from the inside out, to have the Spirit living inside of us, renewing us, refreshing us and reviving us. The only requirement is that we've got to get real—to be authentic and transparent enough to name the counterfeits in our lives, acknowledge that they're not working to meet our needs and bring them back to Jesus to exchange them for the real thing that only he can supply.

BE AUTHENTIC AND
TRANSPARENT IN WORSHIP

The woman said to him, "Sir, I see that you are a prophet. Our ancestors worshiped on this mountain, but you [Jews] say that the place where people must worship is in Jerusalem." Jesus said to her, "Woman, believe me, the hour is coming when you will worship the Father neither on this mountain nor in Jerusalem. You [Samaritans] worship what you do not know; we worship what we know, for salvation is from the Jews. But the hour is coming, and is now here, when the true worshipers will worship the Father in spirit and truth."

JOHN 4:19-23

I was first introduced to InterVarsity Christian Fellowship as a new believer at Rutgers University. I was looking for a group I could belong to that would help me to grow in my newfound faith. On my first visit, I entered a room filled with white students. I felt somewhat out of place but resolved to stay and get as much out of the Bible study as I could. After a brief time of worship in which a young man led us in songs with his guitar (songs I had never heard before in my life!), another student stood up and invited us all to join him in the front of the room for prayer. As I went forward to pray with all the others, we were asked to give prayer requests, and then we were instructed to pray for the various things that were mentioned.

I was excited to participate in a part of the worship experience that I felt I was good at. I came from an exuberant black church tradition in which prayer was a primary focus. It was a common experience for us to stay at church and pray all night long for the needs of our families, community and church. We would all gather around the altar, and in one voice we would bombard heaven with our heartfelt prayers. It was a powerful time, and many people testified to the miraculous ways that God answered their prayers.

As I stood in the front of the auditorium with the InterVarsity group, memories of these good times of prayer swelled in my heart. I eagerly waited for the chance to connect with my new Christian brothers and sisters in prayer. When the time came to pray, I lifted my hands, closed my eyes and started praying out loud with all the sincerity that I could muster. I prayed for one request after the other in the mighty name of Jesus.

But after a few minutes I realized that no one else was praying except me. Opening my eyes, to my embarrassment I saw everyone in the room staring at me in disbelief! I immediately felt awkward and out of place. I stopped praying and listened as the other students prayed in what I later learned was a "conversational prayer" style. Each person voiced a short prayer, and then someone else would follow and agree in prayer.

After the prayer time was over, I stayed for the rest of the meeting, but I never attended another large group meeting of InterVarsity on my campus. No one had been outwardly hostile to me. In fact, most people had been pleasant, but I just didn't feel I fit in. As a result of that one negative experience, a gap grew between us, and we didn't know how to bridge the divide. That night I learned that differences in worship can divide well-meaning Christians and compromise our ability to work together as witnesses of the gospel.

BRIDGING THE RELIGIOUS DIVIDE

There was a history of division between the Samaritans and the Jews regarding worship. The Samaritans considered themselves descendants of Jacob but were completely pagan in their religious practices. At first they worshiped the idols of the nations they had come from. There was, however, a spate of attacks by mountain lions, which had increased greatly while the land of northern Israel was uninhabited, and the people supposed it was because they had not honored the God of that geographic region (see 2 Kings 17:24-29). A Jewish priest was therefore sent to them from Babylon to instruct them in the Jewish religion, and they incorporated the worship of Yahweh—the God of Israel—along with their idolatry. They also obtained permission to build a temple on Mount Gerizim, which the Jews viewed to be in opposition to their temple in Jerusalem. Although the Samaritans acknowledged the divine authority of the law of Moses, they rejected the writings of the prophets and all the Jewish traditions. The Samaritans vehemently argued that Mount Gerizim was the place designated by Moses as the place where the nation should worship. This fueled an irreconcilable hatred between the two groups, and the Jews refused to have any fellowship with the Samaritans.

The conversation between the woman and Jesus triggers her memory of this age-old dispute between the Jews and the Samaritans. Jesus acknowledges her grievance and assures her that the day is coming when worship will transcend such religious divisions. Instead of being defined by religious rituals and practices, true worship will be distinguished by authenticity, transparency and openness of being. Jesus explains that "the true worshipers will worship the Father in the Spirit and truth." In fact, he makes it clear that the Father is searching for people who worship like this—people who are "naked and unashamed" before God and others as it was said of the first humans, Adam and Eve, in Genesis 1. I believe that what Jesus is saying is "This is what it means to worship—to be honest about who you really are in the presence of God. It means to present your true self to God, knowing that you are created in his image and are loved unconditionally." Worship is therefore to be your true self—the person that God created you to be—without pretense. God is looking for people who truthfully acknowledge that they can't change or transform themselves. When we come into the presence of God, we don't come as perfect people but as needy people who, despite our best efforts, know that we can't fully satisfy the longings of our soul. Therefore we refuse to be conformed to this world and how it thinks but we present ourselves as living sacrifices before God, which is our reasonable act of worship according to Romans 12:1-2.

When we worship in this way, it doesn't matter whether we raise our hands or whether we fall down on our knees, because the form becomes insignificant to the truth. It is in worship that God calls us out of the shadows of our shame, our insecurities and our pretense to tell us who we really are. It is in his presence that we are empowered to exchange the counterfeit for the real thing so that we can become our true selves. In this place of spiritual authenticity, honesty vulnerability and transparency, we experience an ongoing conversion process that validates our claim to be followers of Jesus. Wherever this occurs around the world, human differences are transcended and people who are thirsty find God.

When we fail to worship God in this way, however, we will inadvertently fall into some form of idolatry that produces divisions and schisms that damage our credibility. As Rick Richardson says,

> Human beings were made to worship. We will worship something or someone, whether God, other gods, the law, created things, other men or other women, sexuality, science, technology, our own rational mind, our cultural background or identity, our consciousness or ourselves. Humans will worship. Sin at its heart is idolatry, not ac-

knowledging God as God but worshiping created things instead of God. Once we choose to worship other things in the place of God, our understanding becomes darkened and our lives become confused.

When this occurs, worship is no longer a unifying force but becomes a divisive experience that drives people apart. Then our conversations about Christ are not attractive to non-Christians, because they disintegrate into debates about religious rules, regulations and denominational differences.

THE UNIFYING POWER OF WORSHIP

Engaging in an ancient religious feud did not distract Jesus from the real issue at hand with the woman at the well. He had not come to debate theological differences that drive a wedge between people. True worship, in which we see ourselves for who we are—people who are all in desperate need of a Savior—breaks down barriers between people and creates common ground. The saying "The ground is level at the foot of the cross" is true. There are no perfect people. We are all sinners, imperfect people, beggars who are in need of bread. When we come to the Communion table in worship to remember the sacrificial death of Christ, we recognize that we all need the transforming power of God to change our lives. We also acknowledge that we are brothers and sisters, members of the same family, and we need each other to survive, regardless of our racial, ethnic, cultural or denominational differences.

As I have talked to many people about their views about Christianity, I have learned that they are hungry for an authentic spiritual experience and are tired of seeing a church marked by divisions of ethnicity, social class, denomination and doctrine. If we Christians would take seriously their concerns, we could establish our credibility as witnesses of the gospel by being an example of a unified worshiping community made up of people from "every tribe and nation," as described in Revelation 7:9. This would be a powerful witness to the world, and worship would become an attractive force for evangelism. In Richardson's words, "Genuine worship is especially helpful in evangelism today because it can be an authentic experience of the reality of God in community." I saw this happen at a conference of 450 college students in Portland, Oregon, sponsored by InterVarsity Christian Fellowship. Ten students committed their lives to Jesus. One young man later e-mailed me to share what had happened for him during the worship:

> On Saturday night of the conference I was standing on a chair over-looking a crowd of Asian, African-American, Latino and White students worshiping God to the sound of a Native American band. The tribal drums and worshipers from all ethnicities escorted God's presence into the room. God's presence in the room that night was profound and blessed the people. I was moved and prayed to become part of the kingdom. I gave my life to God and became a Christian that night.
>
> On Sunday towards the end of the conference you stopped preaching and began to call on someone from the audience. This person, you said, "was a male and had given himself to God the previous night." That person was me. It was a powerful experience. I proclaim God, that he is the one and only almighty God. He sought me out even when I have major setbacks.

What a powerful testimony! I believe that many other people are looking for a similar authentic experience of God in the context of community. The Christian community could be that place if we could put aside our differences and submit our traditions to a higher kingdom agenda.

It doesn't matter whether you prefer to be sprinkled or submerged in water when you are baptized. Whether you believe in speaking in a heavenly prayer language or not isn't the most important thing. It is not central to the gospel whether you raise your hands in worship or sit silently and reverently in your seat. It is not a deal-breaker if you believe that women should preach or not. But let us covenant together, for the sake of our witness, that we do whatever we do in spirit and in truth. Let's resolve to experience God in a life-changing, transformative way and invite others to do the same.

Show up to worship as your true self, not as a facade behind which you are hiding. Let us not be entangled by our sins, which turn worship into an inauthentic practice devoid of real life-changing power. Remember that after they sinned, Adam and Eve were no longer "naked and unashamed." Instead they hid themselves from the presence of God and from each other because they were afraid, as it says in Genesis 3:8-9; they refused to answer when God asked, "Where are you?"

Let us worship truthfully and answer by saying, "Here I am." Here I am with all my problems, my longings, my questions and my mistakes. Here I am with the things I like about myself and the things I wish I could change. Here I am! I'm not running away, and I'm not hiding from you. I'm not trying to sidestep the issue or engage you in religious debates. Instead I am presenting myself to you—warts and all—and I am asking you to let your kingdom come on earth as it is in heaven, and let it begin with me.

MAKE A LIFE-CHANGING DECISION

The woman said to him, "I know that Messiah is coming" (who is called Christ). "When he comes, he will proclaim all things to us." Jesus said to her, "I am he, the one who is speaking to you."

JOHN 4:25-26

I knew it was getting to be time for me to decide what I really believed and who I actually wanted to be. I had assumed a type of "double agent" lifestyle, and the pretense was becoming more difficult for me to maintain. When I was around my friend Margaret, who was a serious Christian, I asked questions about the faith, watched my language and was generally well behaved. One day she knocked on the door of my dormitory room when I was smoking a cigarette. I quickly threw the cigarette out the window and sprayed a room deodorizer to try to maintain my Christian pretense. However, when Margaret wasn't around and I was with my partygoing friends, I continued to act cool, talk tough, dabble in drugs, date guys who weren't good for me and hang out at discotheques.

The hazards of my lifestyle finally became real for me one night when two of my college girlfriends took me out for my nineteenth birthday to a concert in Jersey City. We sat together and had a great time until a young man sitting next to us asked us a question. He said, "Do you sisters get high?"

Since I didn't know this guy and I had an unspoken, albeit twisted, moral rule that I wouldn't smoke marijuana with someone I didn't know, I didn't answer him. My girlfriends responded positively, and he passed them a joint. They each took a puff and gave it back to this perfect stranger. He asked, "How'd you like it?" I don't remember what they said, but I will never forget what he said. He said, "Yeah, that was the best opium I could find."

I was horrified! I thought, *Opium?!* The only thing that I even vaguely knew about opium was that historically people had smoked this drug in China and many of them died as a result. I couldn't believe it! Once again I knew that I was in way over my head. It frightened me and offended my sense of right and wrong that people didn't play by my rules. That night I knew that this life was not the life for me, that sooner or later it would kill me and that I had to get out of it before it was too late. I had no more excuses, and now I was just waiting for the right time.

NO MORE EXCUSES

That's exactly where my friend Sam finds herself in this unplanned meeting with Jesus. She has tried to debate social, cultural and religious issues, and that has not worked to take the focus off of her and her thirst for something more in life. So she says to Jesus, "I know that Messiah is coming. When he comes, he will proclaim all things to us." Basically what she is saying is, I don't have any more excuses but I'm not ready to make a decision yet. I want to wait until the Messiah comes. When he comes, he will explain everything to us, but right now I'm not ready.

Jesus said to her what he says to each one of us: The person you're waiting for, the one who will explain everything to you—I am he. I am the one, says Jesus, who can make sense out of your life. I am the one who can satisfy your thirst. I am the one who can answer all your questions. Whoever you are, wherever you live, whatever your name is and no matter what you've done, Jesus declares, "I'm the One you have been looking for."

Real Christianity is not a religion; it's a relationship with Jesus. He gives us internal resources that nurture us, replenish us and give us life—not from the outside in but from the inside out. Everything that my friend Sam tried to do to fill the hole in her soul has been external, and it hasn't worked. Jesus offers her a way to stop looking outside of herself for peace, purpose and happiness. Instead, he will give the water that will become a permanent inner well that has the power to satisfy her deepest thirsts.

To access this "living water" Sam must be willing to make a decision to exchange counterfeit, inadequate methods for the real thing that only Jesus can supply. This is where many people run into difficulty. I know because it happened to me.

MY DECISION

It was the last Friday night in October 1974 when I came face to face with my need to make a decision. I was home for the weekend, visiting my family, and my small Pentecostal church was having a series of special services called a revival. My mother, who was a member of a more prestigious Baptist church, had never attended my church with me, so I invited her to come to the revival. She agreed.

For the most part the worship service was exactly what I was accustomed to and expected. My mother and I sat together about seven rows from the front of the church. There was great singing, powerful praying and testimonies about the goodness of God. However, there was something I was not prepared for. Although my church was a place of powerful experiential faith, it was not known for the depth of its expository preaching and teaching. On that night I was impressed by how articulate and insightful the guest speaker was. He was an outstanding communicator of biblical truth.

At the conclusion of his sermon he gave a prophecy—an extemporaneous word from God that gives insight or foresight into a specific matter of human affairs. Although I had been impressed by his sermon, today I don't remember what he said. But I can still remember the exact prophetic words that he spoke afterward. He said, "There is a young person here tonight who's toddling the fence. You're on one side of the fence at one time and on the other side of the fence at another. God wants you to make a decision for him tonight."

I said to myself, *He can't be talking about me; he must be talking about the other obviously unsaved young people, because I've been thinking about getting myself together.*

He responded to my unspoken thought by saying out loud, "Yes, I'm talking about you—the person who just said to themselves, *Is he talking about me?*"

Now I was shocked and terrified! I did not want my mother and all the Christian people of my church, who thought that I was so good, to know about the kind of life I had been living. So I sat there, sweating it out.

Finally a woman right in front of me stood up. I was relieved—but the evangelist, Luther Blackwell, said, "No daughter, it's not you. God has shown me who you are, but I'm not at liberty to call you out. This is a decision that you have to make for yourself tonight—and we're not going to wait all night for you do it. We'll give you two minutes." He looked at his watch and began to count down the time: "A minute fifty-five seconds. Won't you come? One minute thirty seconds. The Bible says, 'The day you hear my voice, harden not your heart.' One minute. Don't let it be said, 'Too late, too late.' " On and on he went until he finally said, "Time's up. Young lady—yes, it was a young lady—the Lord has instructed me to tell you that you're going to be like Jonah tonight—downhill all the way."

I can't adequately describe the panic I felt! Afterward I didn't want to talk or socialize with people. I couldn't wait to get home. I stayed up and prayed all night. I hardly knew anything about the story of Jonah in the Old Testament. I vaguely remembered that a whale ate Jonah, so I thought that I had committed the unpardonable sin by not responding and that at some point in the near future God was going to kill me! So all night long I prayed one simple but sincere prayer: "Oh God, don't kill me!"

Only later did I realize that I didn't know what to actually do to become a Christian. Although I had attended church all my life, that night in my desperation all I could do was cry. No one had ever clearly explained to me the simple way to salvation or the process of conversion. I didn't know what to do!

On Sunday evening I returned to my campus and couldn't wait to talk to Margaret. I went to her room eager to find out everything about the book of Jonah that she could tell me. Another friend was there visiting at the time. His name is Theodore A. Faison, but everyone called him Tag. He was the only other young Christian person I knew. I told them everything that had happened at church on Friday night, including the prophecy about my impending doom. Margaret read the small book of Jonah with me over and over again. Finally she said, "Brenda, Jonah was in trouble with God until he did what God wanted him to do. You're going to have to decide what God wants you to do—and do it."

I knew exactly what that was. It was time for me to make a decision to accept the gift of a new life that was being offered to me through Jesus Christ. After I returned to my own room, Tag came by to make sure that I was okay. Together we knelt and prayed. Without any fanfare, tears or any other outward display of emotion, I sincerely invited Jesus into my life. I gave him permission to change me and to rewrite my story.

It was a life-changing decision and one that I have never regretted. More than thirty years since I made that choice, and I can truthfully say, beyond a shadow of a doubt, that it was the best decision I have ever made in my life!

WHEN JESUS SHOWS UP

So welcome to the well! The well is the place where we meet Jesus and we meet others at their point of need, just as Tag met me when I needed to make a decision. The well is the place where people are called to make life-changing decisions. The well is the place where Jesus shows up unexpectedly and keeps a personal appointment. The well is the place where Jesus changes the script and rewrites the narrative of each of our lives to give us a story worth living for.

If you are tired of business as usual—of a life that doesn't work the way you wish it did or of a partial presentation of the gospel story that doesn't really work in the world we live in—then this is the place for you. This is the place where followers of Jesus take deliberate steps toward the kingdom of God.

Today many people can't envision an inclusive kingdom community where people from different backgrounds live together in peace. There are no successful models to refer to, so they don't believe us anymore when we talk about it. Some years ago I read a moving article by a young woman named Sarah E. Hinlicky, who makes this point very clearly:

> We can't even imagine a world of cultural or national unity; our world is more like a tattered patchwork quilt. We have every little inconsequential thing . . . homepages and cell phones, but not one important thing to believe in. What do you have left to persuade us? One thing: the story. We are story people. We know narratives, not ideas. Our surrogate parents were the TV and the VCR, and we can spew out entertainment trivia at the drop of a hat. We treat our ennui with stories, more and more stories, because they are the only thing to make sense; when the external stories fail, we make a story of our own lives. You wonder why we're so self-destructive, but we're looking for the one story with staying power, the destruction and redemption of our own lives. That's to your advantage: you have the best redemption story on the market.

Stories connect us to others and give meaning to our existence. Jesus calls us to share our testimony with others in just the way Hinlicky suggests. We have to resist the urge to be churchy and just be real about where we've come from and who we are now—even as Jesus continues to redeem us. This authenticity is what will call people to decision.

That's what Jesus offers us at the well—a "plot worth living." Jesus is offering a way to find meaning for our lives in a world that is fragmented by ethnic, gender, age and social class divisions. He is providing a way for people to experience real Christianity—the story that offers hope for the future. However, to embrace this we will need to exchange our outdated, culturally conditioned ideas and methods that limit the power and effectiveness of the gospel. We have a message that is more powerful and compelling than the realities that we face. We have been entrusted with the greatest story ever told. What Jesus wants to offer the world through us is a way for people to bring their stories into interaction with God's story, so that they can have a new storyline full of purpose, meaning and hope.

10

TAKE ACTION TO BE COUNTERCULTURAL

Just then his disciples came. They were astonished that he was speaking with a woman, but no one said, "What do you want?" or, "Why are you speaking with her?"

JOHN 4:27

My husband, Derek, had the opportunity to go to India with a team of other professors and graduate students from Wheaton College. They had been asked to train Indian evangelists in basic listening and counseling skills. In India he met a dedicated group of indigenous evangelists called Master Trainers, who commit themselves to two months of theological and practical training so they can go to remote areas and preach the gospel. Their purpose is to introduce new converts to Christ and to raise up other leaders as future evangelists.

This is a holistic approach to evangelism that is based on meeting the needs of the people through subsistence farming. The evangelists teach people how to farm and cultivate the land to meet their very real need for food. The evangelists are accepted as a valuable part of the community because they provide a useful and necessary service.

Further, the founder of the ministry employs non-Christians and people from different castes to work at the training facility to serve in various capacities such as cooks or drivers. This brings them into the community of faith where they can see the gospel lived out and experience the reality of God's love and care for them in everyday, practical, life-saving ways. In this context words of proclamation about Jesus and the kingdom of God follow readily, because through their social action these Christians have won the right to speak their truth.

BREAKING RULES

Jesus broke every rule in the book when he conversed with the Samaritan woman! He broke religious rules, cultural norms and social standards. As a rabbi he was forbidden to teach the law to a woman; as a Jew he shouldn't be caught dead with a Samaritan; as a man he risked his own personal and moral reputation if he spoke with a woman of ill repute. This was extremely problematic for Jesus, because he was already in trouble with the religious leaders of his day, who claimed the authority to regulate the rites and ceremonies of their religion. They supposed that they had the right to monitor Jesus' activities, and they discovered that he was growing in popularity with the people because he was baptizing more disciples than John the Baptist. Those in authority were displeased and threatened by Jesus' success, probably because by drawing many away after him he weakened their authority and influence. They were looking for a reason to discredit and punish him.

So when the disciples returned from going into the city to buy food, they were shocked and extremely displeased to find Jesus conversing with the Samaritan woman. The Scripture text says in John 4:27 that when his disciples came "they were astonished that he was speaking with a woman, but no one said, 'What do you want?' or, 'Why are you speaking with her?'"

They knew the social, cultural and religious expectations of their day. Fathers were forbidden to teach their daughters the law, and rabbis did not discuss religious matters with women. Even though none of the disciples voiced concern at what their rabbi was doing, their disapproving stares, their frowns and the unkind expressions on their faces told the whole story of their confusion and displeasure.

This may be an appropriate place to discuss the importance of nonverbal cues and body language in evangelism. Have you ever seen people who looked as if they were wondering why you were talking to a certain person? If so, you know that the look on their faces can say far more than the words that come out of their mouths. That's why it's important to be aware of our body language and facial expressions when sharing the gospel with others—especially in crosscultural situations. People pick up on many more facial and environmental cues than we may realize, and the negative messages they perceive in our body language can severely hinder our efforts at evangelism and reconciliation.

Moreover, it may be better to wait until your friends and family are not around to engage a person from a different background with the message of the kingdom. Even though they may not intend to, your loved ones can ruin your attempts to be a credible witness of the gospel because they are unable to manage their crosscultural discomfort. There is a very real phenomenon called a *crowd mentality,* and the disapproval of the people who are with us can cause others to distrust us or doubt our credibility.

In addition, the disapproving looks and biased advice of our family and friends can adversely affect our choices and behavior. They can weaken our resolve to be a kingdom person who demonstrates the truth and power of the gospel to break down the dividing walls between people. Often they have no malice—they love us. They are afraid and don't want us to get hurt or cause trouble, so they try to dissuade us by saying things like "It's not a wise career move. It might hurt your academic or professional advancement if you become too radical about this." Or people in our local church might caution us by saying, "I really care for you, and I don't think that it is a good idea for you to buy a house in *that* community, because it's not safe."

However, Jesus' style of evangelism doesn't follow accepted social rules—even the rules of the evangelical community. And like Jesus, we must be willing to break unjust laws and take action that is counter to the culture around us in order to regain credibility in the world. There will be times when Jesus will call us to go against the status quo. There will be some things that Jesus will call us to do for the gospel that will not be popular or comfortable. This calling might take us away from the people who love us and are trying their best to keep us safe. We will have to decide that the mandate of God on our lives calls us to make a commitment, and sometimes we might have to stand alone.

Sometimes in order to really pursue the kingdom of God, we're going to have to break some rules. We're going to have to go where we're not supposed to go and do what we're not supposed to do. It's called civil disobedience. Every now and then we're going to have to be unpopular, we're going to have to get in trouble.

So for your sake and for the sake of the person you are trying to reach, you may want to establish your credibility away from the crowd in a place where you can be honest and vulnerable and where the other person won't have to feel the judgment of the people who came with you.

UNPOPULAR PREACHING

I can remember the first time I preached about racial reconciliation in an all black church. It was not altogether well received. People were used to hearing me preach about spiritual life issues and then offer an evangelistic altar call that didn't mention social justice or global realities. When I started preaching about racial reconciliation, they wondered when I was going to go back to the way I used to preach. They wrongly assumed that the only point of preaching about reconciliation was to tell white people what they had to do to make restitution for the injustices done to black people in America. However, my message also challenged African Americans to become more interculturally competent and to commit ourselves to understanding other ethnic groups, learning to speak Spanish, and interacting with Asian American people, Native American people and people from other countries. This was not a popular message, and some of the churches that used to invite me regularly to speak don't have me come as often as before.

Sometimes when we take countercultural social action it will get us into trouble—even with people from our own culture. However, if we are going to close the credibility gap between what the gospel says and how we live as Christians, we will have to step out of the box and break some rules. We will have to preach some unpopular messages, and people in our congregations will wonder, "When is Pastor going to go back to what he's supposed to be preaching? He's not supposed to be preaching about reconciliation or about engaging the culture around us. We're not interested in this. When is he going to go back to preaching the Bible?"

We should be ready for this kind of criticism when we embrace real Christianity. It will take a firm resolve that is rooted and anchored in our clear understanding of the gospel. It won't be easy, because we will be going against the grain of how this world thinks and operates. That's why the apostle Paul admonishes us in Romans 12:1-2, "I urge you, brothers and sisters, in view of God's mercy, to offer your bodies as a living sacrifice, holy and pleasing to God—this is true worship. Do not conform to the pattern of this world, but be transformed by the renewing of your mind. Then you will be able to test and approve what God's will is—his good, pleasing and perfect will" (TNIV).

DEMONSTRATING THE GOSPEL

The kingdom of God is not of this world, and to be credible representatives of it we must be willing to take countercultural social action. Jesus did more than talk about reconciliation and crossing barriers—he did it! He took literal steps of action to bridge the gap and establish his credibility with the Samaritan woman.

This is exactly what we are called to do as Christ-followers. In this postmodern world people need an experiential truth that goes beyond the words we speak. If we want to influence this experience-oriented generation with the gospel, we cannot just talk about peace, unity and reconciliation—we must demonstrate it. This means that we must practice what we preach and put our words into action. This has implications for how we live day to day. Our gospel should influence the way we vote. We should choose candidates who would help move us toward the kingdom values of peace and reconciliation. If we are leaders of an organization, our institutional policies and corporate practices should reflect reconciliation as a witness to our Christian faith. Remember the words of James: "Faith by itself, if it is not accompanied by action, is dead" (2:17 NIV). Our faith has no real life if we don't act on it. This seems to imply that we must validate our belief in the gospel with corresponding actions. We have to practice our faith in ways that verify our credibility as a follower of Christ.

The results may not always be popular, and at times we may have to incur the anger and displeasure of those we care for because we have challenged the social conditions around us. Such was the case with Martin Luther King Jr., who broke the rules and was jailed for his opposition to injustice. In his famous "Letter from a Birmingham Jail," Dr. King explained to other ministers why taking action was necessary:

> You may well ask: "Why direct action? Why sit-ins, marches and so forth? Isn't negotiation a better path?" You are quite right in calling, for negotiation. Indeed, this is the very purpose of direct action. Nonviolent direct action seeks to create such a crisis and foster such a tension that a community, which has constantly refused to negotiate, is forced to confront the issue. It seeks so to dramatize the issue that it can no longer be ignored. My citing the creation of tension as part of the work of the nonviolent-resister may sound rather shocking. But I must confess that I am not afraid of the word

"tension." I have earnestly opposed violent tension, but there is a type of constructive, nonviolent tension which is necessary for growth. Just as Socrates felt that it was necessary to create a tension in the mind so that individuals could rise from the bondage of myths and half-truths to the unfettered realm of creative analysis and objective appraisal, we must see the need for nonviolent gad-flies to create the kind of tension in society that will help men rise from the dark depths of prejudice and racism to the majestic heights of understanding and brotherhood.

This stand taken by Dr. King—a Christian minister—so many years ago is still having impact on our society today. Recently I read an article titled "Why I Hate Blacks" that was published on an Asian American web-site. Written by an Asian man, it featured blatantly racist and stereotypical comments about African Americans—deeply offensive statements. More noteworthy than this, however, were the Asian American leaders who criticized the website for allowing such an article to be published. One leader wrote, "Most Asian Americans would not be here in America today, but for the civil rights movement led by African Americans that resulted in the change to racist immigration quotas." Another leader said, "Asian Americans should recognize the debt we all owe African Americans who blazed the civil rights path we have walked on in our journey to equality." These comments and the many others I read in response to the article are an indication that the direct action we take to demonstrate the gospel can have a far-reaching impact on the lives of others in ways we may be un-able to anticipate. This is why we must expand our understanding of evangelism to embrace a holistic model that goes beyond words to in-clude active engagement in the world around us.

11

BE A BRIDGE BUILDER

Then the woman left her water jar and went back to the city. She said to the people, "Come and see a man who told me everything I have ever done! He cannot be the Messiah, can he?" They left the city and were on their way to him.

JOHN 4:28-30

Anne is a natural bridge builder. She is a beautiful Christian woman who has a deep heart to cross the boundaries that divide people from each other. I think that her life has prepared her for this important role. Her great-grandfather came to the United States from China, and he and his wife had nine children. Her grandfather was one of the children born into this family. Everyone in his generation speaks Cantonese, but his daughter—Anne's mother—and the relatives born in her generation were Westernized and all speak English. Most of them did not marry Chinese people, and therefore most of their children are biracial. Anne is no exception, but instead of being of white and Chinese parentage like most of her cousins, she has a combined African American and Chinese heritage. Anne does not look as Chinese as her cousins do, and throughout her life she has struggled to establish the fact that she is really Chinese. Over the years it has been difficult for Anne to deal with curious stares and comments from strangers. Since she was a child people have questioned her identity, and those who are Chinese have challenged her ethnicity by saying things like "You're not Chinese. You don't look Chinese. You're only half." The inherent message in their harsh words is "You are not one of us. You don't look like us. So don't try to claim us." Consequently Anne, like many other biracial people, has struggled with her ethnic identity all of her life. Reflecting on how these comments made her feel, Anne says, "Everyone wants to be whole. Everyone wants to be 100 percent. Hearing those things didn't make me feel complete. I felt like I was not Chinese enough to be considered Chinese or black enough to be fully embraced by African Americans. Black people made me choose to identify with them or I was considered a 'sellout.' I didn't know what box to check when asked about my racial heritage. I didn't fit in anywhere. It made me feel very insecure."

Although these experiences were extremely hurtful, Anne experienced the greatest pain of racism in her own family. Members of the family chose to disinherit her mother, and her parents were disrespected. When Anne was small, her grandfather would not hug her or hold her hand in public. Once when they were in a store she called him Grandpa and he didn't answer or acknowledge her. He acted as if she was not with him. It was always a strain to go out in public.

Recently Anne and her husband made a major decision: she and her three children would visit her parents for six months. Anne's grandfather is now ninety-two years old. He is very sick and weak and needs to be cared for. Her mother and father, who are both Christians, have been living with him as his full-time caregivers. Since her father's health is also failing, Anne would be helping her mother with the hard job of caring for both of them. Prior to her visit Anne prayed that God would open up her grandfather's heart and soften him. She went in a spirit of forgiveness and reconciliation.

After the years of her parents' consistent care for him and Anne's loving posture, one day her grandfather went to a restaurant for dim sum with Anne and her children. He introduced them to his friends and bragged about them. He is proud of his great-grandchildren and how well they have embraced their Chinese culture. An older aunt, who had once disowned her mother, lovingly pinched Anne's daughter's cheeks in public and said she was beautiful. These experiences brought much healing for Anne and her parents.

Looking back over these past months, Anne says, "This trip has been life changing. I've grown in knowing who I am in Christ. No longer is it important to me to be that or this." She and her parents have loved people in spite of how they were treated. As a result they are sharing the gospel as credible witnesses of Jesus Christ. Because of their forgiveness and reconciliation, many people have asked questions like "What do you have in your life that helps you love like this? It has to be more than just you being a nice person." Some friends and family members have taken notice of their example and lifestyle and are starting to believe in Jesus. One Chinese cousin has begun to attend church with Anne and her children because she is impressed with the genuine reconciliation happening between Anne, her parents and her grandfather. A young Russian woman has recommitted her life to Christ and now regularly attends church with Anne; she also reads her Bible daily and has paid off her credit cards because she is really trying to live a life that that is pleasing to God. She says that this is because she has seen Anne's life of service and sacrifice.

This is what it means to be a bridge builder—bringing people together as a credible witness of the life-changing difference God has made in our lives.

A LIVING WITNESS OF THE GOSPEL

My friend Sam has had a life-changing experience with Jesus Christ. When his disciples returned, she could sense their displeasure, so she abruptly left her water jar and hurried back to her town. When she got there, she told other Samaritans about her experience with Jesus and urged them to come and investigate him for themselves. Although her people had ostracized her, she was now living in the dignity and sense of worth that have come from her direct encounter with Jesus. So she became an evangelist and said, "I just met a man who told me everything that I have ever done. There is something unusual about him. He is not like the other Jews. He seems to be authentic. I believe him, and I think that he might actually be who he says he is—the Christ. Come! Check him out. Come experience him for yourselves. I believe he could actually be the Messiah!"

This is a wonderful example of how the gospel of the kingdom spreads to unlikely places and unlikely people. We need those who, like the Samaritan woman, have experienced the reconciling power of God to go back into their communities as living witnesses of the gospel. We all have relational ties and familial connections that give us access to certain groups of people. There are some places where certain people can go because of their relationships, ethnic heritage or ability to speak the language that other people may not have entree into. In addition, there are some people who might never listen to someone else but will listen to you because they know you and trust your judgment. There may be colleagues, friends and family members who will listen to and believe your story when they doubt the credibility of other Christians. When you speak they might actually listen; therefore if you cross the boundaries of race, ethnicity, age, gender and social class for the sake of gospel, they might seriously consider it also.

We need more Christians who will go back to their own communities and say, "We need to hear this message. We need to understand that there are both vertical and horizontal dimensions to the cross that we must embrace. If we want our church, our group or our institution to be a credible witness of the gospel in this present generation, we will have to experience and proclaim the whole truth of God's kingdom."

We also become bridge builders when we partner with people from different backgrounds as a visible witness to our unity through Jesus Christ. This might mean inviting someone of a different gender, political persuasion, age or nationality to teach your group. If you are a person of influence in your company or institution, you could suggest a particular book for your colleagues to read that they may not have otherwise considered.

Our credibility as Christians is enhanced and people are drawn to Jesus Christ when we cross barriers to bridge the gaps that divide people. Pastor Bill Hybels of Willow Creek Community Church, an outstanding "seeker-sensitive" congregation outside Chicago, says, "I believe that ten out of ten people would agree that when they boil down their salvation experience, it always involved one person making a decision to walk toward them and reach out a hand of friendship. Someone taking a risk for them to bridge an ethnic, religious, or socioeconomic chasm." This is what it means to be a bridge builder, and these are the steps we can take that could change someone's life.

DO THE RIGHT THING

In order for our credibility to be established in a new community, we often need bridge people who will vouch for us. As my friend Sam did for Jesus, we need others who will speak for our integrity and authenticity. The Samaritan woman bridged Jesus to her people by sharing her personal experience and telling her story.

This reminds me of a movie I saw years ago, *Do the Right Thing* by director Spike Lee. In this film there are two brothers of Italian ethnicity. Their father owns a pizzeria in Bedford-Stuyvesant, New York, and although they grew up in that community, their family has long since moved out. However, every day these two brothers come back with their dad to help manage the business. The demographics of the neighborhood have changed dramatically. As businesses have moved out, poor black and Hispanic people have moved in, and now the community is only a shadow of its former self.

The two brothers have two totally different reactions to working in this inner-city community. One brother hates it, and every day that he comes to work he is disgruntled. He begs his father to "sell the place" because he hates coming to work there and having to be with "those people." He stays inside the pizzeria and never mingles with the neighbors. He spends his days in agony, hoping that he'll soon be able to leave that neighborhood and not have to continue working in what he felt was such a horrible place.

The second brother takes a different approach: he decides to become a bridge builder. He makes friends with the delivery boy who works for his father. Spike Lee plays this character, whose name is Mookie. They share stories and joke with each other as they hang out together. One day Mookie and this young Italian American venture into the community, beyond the boundaries of the pizzeria. As they walk down the street, three young black men approach them. The leader of the group is nicknamed Buggin'-Out, and he fits the description because his hair is wildly uncombed and stands all over his head. As Buggin'-Out and his two ominous-looking friends approach Mookie and his companion, they began to taunt the white guy: "What you doing on our street, white boy? Get off our sidewalk and get out our neighborhood! We don't want you here." At this point in the movie Mookie speaks up and says to Buggin'-Out, "Yo man, don't mess with him. He's down." Not dissuaded, they continue to shove him and taunt him. Once again Mookie stands up and says, "Yo, man, I'm telling you, don't mess with him—he's down."

Now Mookie is being a bridge builder. What he is saying is "I can vouch for him. He's authentic. I can attest to his credibility. I can't speak for his brother, and I can't speak for every other white person, but I can speak for him. He is real and genuine. Don't bother him or lump him into the same category with all other white people, because I've tested his heart. I've seen who he really is. This guy can be trusted, and he is worthy to be in our neighborhood. He's my friend. I will stand up for him."

We need more bridge builders like Mookie and the Samaritan woman who will do the right thing. Bridge builders are people who are willing to extend themselves in relationship to connect with those who have been viewed as the "other." In doing this, they risk rejection from those they have extended themselves to and the possibility of alienation from their own group. They take this risk to act as a covering so that credibility can be established. In order to share the gospel with people who are different from us, we need those who can attest to our credibility and authenticity. These bridge people must know that we have honored their culture and respected their differences so they will feel confident in bringing us into their community. As we are invited in, we have opportunities to share the living water that Jesus has given to us.

As Hybels says with eloquence,

> Living water exists inside of Christ-followers not only that your eternal thirst might be quenched, but also that you would walk into work each day choosing to be focused on more than just the "business at hand." That you would be tender toward the Spirit's prompt to cross an office complex or a construction site or a school building. That you would remember Christ's blood, shed for each and every person you see. That you would put some action behind your faith as you cross a room, look a person directly in the eyes, and ask, "Would you like a cup of water?"

There are many people who are thirsty to hear the good news about Jesus and his kingdom. They will be far more receptive to hearing the gospel from someone they trust. Credibility wins trust.

As people bridge us to their community and vouch for our credibility, it can open the door for us to speak or have influence in places that may have dismissed us in the past. We need bridge builders like the Samaritan woman who will say, "I believe God is using this person, and they have something to say that we need to hear."

You or your organization might be the bridge that other people are waiting for. It could be because of your testimony, your experience, your connections or your influence that others are given the opportunity to experience Jesus for themselves.

May it be said of us as it was of the Samaritan woman in John 4:39-42, "Many Samaritans from that city believed in him because of the woman's testimony, 'He told me everything I have ever done.' . . . They said to the woman, 'It is no longer because of what you said that we believe, for we have heard for ourselves, and we know that this is truly the Savior of the world.'" May many people come into the kingdom of God because they have seen our lives and find us credible witnesses of the gospel that we preach.

CONCLUSION

Taking the Witness Stand
with J. Derek McNeil

My journey to become a global Christian began on my trip to Oxford, England. Dr. Bill Pannell had invited my husband and me to be on a team from Fuller Seminary to lecture on the black church in America. The Oxford Center for Missiological Studies asked us to come because the Anglican Church was declining in urban contexts. Beautiful church buildings were being left vacant due to a lack of attendance. When this occurred, a church was said to be a "redundant church." Research suggested that the decline was due in part to shifting demographic trends caused by increased globalization, industrialization and urbanization. Our sponsors had done research on urban churches and found that the black church in America seemed to excel in dealing with these challenges. Consequently, we were invited to share our insights into the African American church.

Our audience was students and faculty from various countries around the world. On the day that my husband lectured, he spoke about the family in the black church. During his presentation he said that the black church no longer needed the white church in America to survive. He persuasively explained that after centuries of trying to be included, African American people developed their own vibrant churches and didn't need to be accepted by European American Christians anymore. His voice and manner took on a strident tone as it revealed a bit of pride.

A Cambridge professor named John Mockford interrupted him: "Wait a minute, lad. Your church is young and agile. Our church has become old and arthritic. We need you to wait up for us."

There was a noticeable silence in the room as these two men faced each other. Derek spoke, but this time with a new level of empathy in his voice: "By asking me to wait up for you, you have just empowered me to be in relationship with you."

It was an amazing moment between these two men, who appeared so different, and for all of us who were watching. Tears welled up in the eyes of both, and one rolled down John Mockford's cheek. He turned to another Brit sitting next to him and said, "This is embarrassing, eh?" The other man simply nodded in agreement.

That day I learned that my story as an African American Christian has global significance and that I could not stay isolated in my own little "holy huddle" if I was going to serve God's kingdom.

MAKING DISCIPLES OF ALL NATIONS

As Christians we are all called to advance the mission of the kingdom of God. Jesus commissioned his followers to make disciples of all nations. This is recorded in Matthew 28:18-20: "All authority in heaven and on earth has been given to me. Go therefore and make disciples of all nations, baptizing them in the name of the Father and of the Son and of the Holy Spirit, and teaching them to obey everything that I have commanded you. And remember, I am with you always, to the end of the age." This is commonly known as the Great Commission, and evangelical Christians believe that it encapsulates the central mission of the church.

The Jews thought that the offer of new life through the Messiah would be limited to their own nation. However, here Jesus made it clear that no people group (*ethnos*) is to be excluded from hearing the gospel and being invited into the household of God. To make this invitation, we must go beyond our segregated social clusters and historical models of evangelism that focused on individual salvation. The kingdom is a movement to make disciples of *all nations* and not just individual converts. Jesus' call to make disciples of all nations is therefore a corporate and cultural mandate. It moves beyond making individual disciples who happen to be of different nations (*ethnos*) to calling people groups who are defined by their differences. While many Christians have accepted the "one person at a time" model, it should be understood that discipleship is God's global movement, empowered by his Spirit, to bring all nations into the kingdom.

These themes are picked up in Acts 1:8, and specific instructions are given to Christ-followers about how to proceed. Jesus says, "You will receive power when the Holy Spirit has come upon you; and you will be my witnesses in Jerusalem, in all Judea and Samaria, and to the ends of the earth." Here Jesus seems to suggest that there is a natural progression regarding where our witness of the gospel takes place. This movement outward also represents increasing challenges and cultural barriers. First, we begin in Jerusalem. This is on our home turf. This is in the place where we are known and are most comfortable. Jerusalem connotes being with the people we are most familiar with—people who are, for the most part, like us. The circle is then widened to include Judea. This is also a place that we are still familiar with, but there are subtle differences in Judea, subgroups and particularities that require acceptance and flexibility. Judea is close to home; however, different lifestyles and cultural strategies that are expressed in this context can expose us to new challenges.

Next, like Jesus, we have to go through Samaria to be his witnesses on earth. This represents the place nearby that is hostile to us. We are naturally reluctant to go to this place because, unlike Jerusalem and Judea, the people there are quite different from us and we don't identify with them. They are "other." Their worldview and points of reference differ from ours. It is the place where there are power differentials. Samaria represents moving outward and experiencing the "otherness" of outsiders who are near us but with whom we do not associate enough to feel a sense of identification.

To be witnesses in Samaria and beyond, we will need to be aware of the complexity of differences around us. This includes a diversity of nationality, gender, social class, age, ethnicity, politics and religious tradition. Jesus calls the Samaritans, who are represented by the woman at the well, to embrace a faith that challenges the old identities of both Jews and Samaritans. It is a faith that transcends their geography, ethnicity, gender and past history. Christ crosses these barriers, but he does not ignore them. To be global Christians and witnesses of the kingdom, we too must move beyond what we know and are comfortable with. This begins in Jerusalem but going through Samaria tests it. Therefore, we cannot fulfill the Great Commission without choosing to go through Samaria. The following diagram illustrates the progressive levels of "otherness" that we must be willing to engage to be credible witnesses of the gospel.

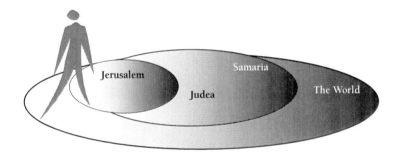

"Samaria" is where we learn how to manage the complexities of otherness so we can extend the call to discipleship to people who are unlike us around the world. Each level that we traverse will require a different set of skills and knowledge to effectively reach people who are different from us with the gospel. After we pass "Judea," where people are still very similar to us, we will need new intercultural competency skills to share the gospel effectively beyond our own people group. As long as we stay in "Jerusalem" or "Judea," we can rely on our own ability to communicate. However, to be effective in making disciples in Samaria and in the rest of the world, we will need to be sensitive to a different system that will require new and different skills, such as adaptive skills, communication skills and interpretative skills. We must also be aware of our cultural identity and history and how it might affect our audience. Jesus was not naive about where he was and to whom he was speaking.

In addition to this, we will need power beyond our own skills and abilities. Jesus instructed his disciples to wait and receive the supernatural power that would mobilize and enable them to take the gospel across religious, ethnic, cultural and social boundaries. Likewise, in order for us to be credible witnesses in the face of globalization and the changes that are occurring all around us, we need the power of the Holy Spirit. This is what happened on the Day of Pentecost as recounted in Acts 2. The Spirit was poured out like fire and empowered the disciples to be effective and bold witnesses of the kingdom. As a result a new multilingual, multiethnic and multinational movement was born, and it became known as the church. People heard the gospel in language so familiar that it sounded like hearing God's message to them in their "mother tongue."

From its inception the Christian church was intended to be a global movement that brings together people from every tribe, language group and nation. In order to be witnesses of this kingdom reality, we must depend upon the power of the Spirit to help us translate the message of the gospel into the language of the context we are communicating in. We must also be empowered to understand and respect the political, economic and cultural realities of these contexts so we can speak the gospel in the "mother tongue" of the people we seek to reach. As on the day of Pentecost, when this happens people are drawn by the power of the Spirit to the truth of gospel, and many are persuaded to become fully devoted followers of Jesus Christ.

BEING WORLD-CLASS CHRISTIANS

I began this book by contending that the authenticity of the message Jesus came to preach about the kingdom is on trial and that the future of our evangelism will rest on how seriously we engage the global postmodern generation with the gospel. One person who has challenged me in my thinking about this is Pastor Robb Thompson of Family Harvest Church in Illinois. He believes that we must make disciples of all nations by training leaders in better government and economic practices based on a Christlike ethic. He is intensely concerned about evangelism and understands that to reach this generation we must engage global leaders who influence the overall society.

People are searching for answers to life's most fundamental questions: Is there anything that can make us feel safe in this world? Why am I here? Is there any real meaning and significance to my life? Why can't people live together in peace? The unsatisfactory answers that have sometimes been given through traditional Christianity have caused some people in the United States to seek answers in places other than the church. Some people have turned to Eastern religious practices, holistic medicine, psychic hotlines, angel worship, or hedonism in a search for meaning and purpose. Despite their aversion to established Christianity, people in their hunger become more open to the transcendent, and this may make them receptive to the message of the gospel after all. It seems that when our world becomes more complex and we feel out of control, we human beings begin to consider our real hunger and thirst for a Power greater than ourselves.

It is into this world that we are called to be a credible witness in defense of the gospel. The "jury" is composed of thirsty people who are seeking for honest answers to complex questions in a changing global society. Through our witness we demonstrate that the kingdom of God is not a figment of our imagination but a reality worth living for. If we seize the opportunity, unbelievers can see that Jesus Christ has once and for all destroyed every barrier that alienated and separated us from God and from each other. Like the Jews and the Samaritans, we can show that God has set us free from our hatred, bigotry, ethnocentrism and fear and made us a new act of creation. We can testify to the fact that we have hope because we are a part of a bigger story that unites the rich and the poor, the incarcerated and the free, the high and the low, males and females, and people from every ethnicity, culture and nation.

Through our proclamation and demonstration of the gospel, we can establish our credibility in this generation. By our actions—both individually and corporately—we can give witness to the fact that sins are forgiven, human divisions are bridged, injustices are set right and imbalances are replaced with equity and reconciliation.

Revelation 21:24-26 gives us a glorious picture of what the ultimate end will be. People from every tribe, language and nation will be gathered before the throne of God, and the kings of the nations will come bearing the glories of their cultures. This is what we are calling people to become disciples of. We have been commissioned to be world-class Christians who are making world-class disciples. It is my prayer that as we live out the principles discussed in this book we will be committed to making disciples of all nations. I can think of no greater privilege than to be active participants with God in causing the kingdom to be more fully realized on earth. Let us therefore give our lives for God's reign to be established, knowing that we are writing the next chapter of the greatest story ever told.

APPENDIX

Leading a Group Discussion

It is my hope that as you embark on leading a discussion about this book's content, you recognize the existence of a credibility gap and are inspired to take steps to close it. As a leader, you have power and influence to lead people closer to the reality of Christ or drive people further away. The credibility of the institution, church or organization that you lead is directly connected to your credibility.

This is an awesome endeavor, and your enthusiasm may well be tempered with feelings of uncertainty or doubt as to how and where to start. It is my intent that this guide be a strategic tool for ministerial or organizational leaders as well as leaders of small groups or teams within ministries, organizations or churches. I believe that it will encourage thoughtful individual reflection, stimulate insightful group discussion and provide practical application tools.

I have organized the guide by chapter. Within each chapter are two sections: one intended at reflective individual work and the other geared toward group discussion and application. We encourage you to get a journal to record your reflections in the individual sections. The story of the woman at the well is a personal story between Jesus and an individual Samaritan woman. Likewise, the work of restoring credibility begins with an individual assessment and ends with an individual conversion process. However, the story does not end on the outskirts of town.

As we all know, the woman ventures into her community and tells everyone she sees about Jesus. Collective social engagement is essential if we are going to close the credibility gap. Accordingly, once you have had a chance to have an internal dialogue regarding the subject matter, there is a group process for which I have given you, the leader, a roadmap.

Each group section begins with questions to facilitate group discussion. Each set of questions is followed by prayer. Prayer is important as recognition and invitation of God's leadership prior to any action. Approach your group prayer time as a dialogue, not a monologue. After you have made your petition, it is important to wait and listen for God to speak before you take any action. I have followed each prayer section with a question or theme for reflection, to focus the group on God's response to each prayer.

Once the group has taken time to seek God about the appropriate action to take in light of the individual reflection and group discussion, it will need ways to apply the new information. The application is offered as a suggested step in the process of restoring our credibility in the world. I urge you to follow the leading of the Holy Spirit in whatever action you take. It is important to *act* and not allow the issues raised to remain a rhetorical discussion. To that end, I have also suggested opportunities for accountability. This work is too important for us to allow each other to get off focus and off track.

I am excited as you embark on this life-changing journey. It is my prayer that as you engage in this process, the result will be transformative for you as a leader and for the community you lead.

CHAPTER 1: KNOW MY CONTEXT TO KNOW MY STORY
Individual Reflection

1. Think about times that persons from particular ethnic or racial groups were defined as being less than equal, or even less than human. Consider the American institution of slavery, internment of Japanese Americans during World War II, the Holocaust, Jim Crow laws, genocide in Rwanda or ethnic cleansing in Bosnia.

In what ways did the cultural definition of persons from these groups as "less than" contribute to the atrocities committed against them?

2. How does the fact that "Sam" was a "double minority" affect the way she was perceived?

Do you think this fact widened or deepened the hole in her soul?

Has there ever been a time when perceptions of the racial, gender or ethnic group to which you belong have affected your own self-esteem and self-worth?

3. In what ways are you or have you been "thirsty"? Where have you gone looking to quench your thirst?

Have you encountered other "thirsty" people who are longing for validation and affirmation? How have you treated them? How does this differ from the way Jesus treated "Sam"?

Group Discussion and Application

1. How did your response to the individual reflection questions cause you to think differently of or to empathize more directly with those of racial, ethnic or gender groups that have been subjected to cultural assault?

2. Have you ever identified certain behaviors of others as "bad" or "sinful" when those individuals were merely trying, albeit in vain, to fill the hole in their soul? Does this change your perception of their actions?

3. How have persons from certain groups in our society been isolated by being declared "unclean"? Who are the modern-day "Samaritans"?

Prayer

God, we give you permission to expose the holes in our souls. Show us the ways we have sought temporary, unsatisfying solutions to the thirst that plagues us. Help us not to judge or condemn others who are acting out of thirst and desperation. Allow us to be whole so that we can be effective in demonstrating your love and acceptance toward those who have been rejected and called "unclean." Guide us as we seek to affirm others and to be loving to those society has deemed unworthy of love. Pour out your creativity through us so that we can find unique ways to counteract the negative messages that many in our society have encountered. Teach us to create atmospheres and spaces where your unconditional love can be manifest so that those who thirst will be thirsty no more. In Jesus' name, amen.

Remember to take some time after prayer to be still and listen for the voice of God speaking to you.

Reflection

What did you hear God say during your time of prayer? What is the action you feel led to take? Are there any prerequisites that must be met before you take action? What are they? What condition must your soul be in before you act?

Application

Choose a group that has been marginalized, called "unclean" and culturally assaulted. Pray about a meaningful way to affirm and bless members of that group. For instance:

• Your church could hold a special celebration honoring women in the faith, or noteworthy Latinos in your community, or African-Americans who have made significant contributions.

• An educational institution could create an exhibit of art from members of such a group.

• A youth ministry could plan a visit to children in the juvenile justice system or the child welfare system. Perhaps the gathering could be a movie night featuring a positive film about a culture group, like *Akeela and the Bee*, *Freedom Writers* or *Take the Lead*, with a discussion following.

Accountability

Once you have agreed on an action, assign a coordinator to lead the charge and set up a timeline for getting it done, keeping in mind that the reason for your action is to provide a counterbalance to the societal and cultural assault on the group you have chosen to affirm.

CHAPTER 2: BEGIN WITH A DIVINE MANDATE
Individual Reflection

1. In what ways have you gone around "Samaria"? Think about the places you have chosen to live, the schools your children attend, the church where you worship. Have you intentionally chosen to remain isolated and insulated in your own community where everyone looks like you?

How is this directly opposite to what Jesus did when he purposely went through Samaria?

2. Do we all have a divine mandate to cross gender lines, racial barriers and denominational divides, or did God just call a few to this kingdom work? Consider your response in light of Luke 3:10.

Group Discussion and Application

1. Have you ever experienced a divine appointment with God? Tell the group about it and discuss.

2. Many times our divine mandate will call us out of our comfort zone and will cause us to be different. Have you ever felt different when choosing to follow God's divine mandate? When? How?

3. Do you see racial reconciliation and ethnic diversity as a divine mandate that comes from Scripture? Why or why not?

Prayer

We ask you, Lord, to examine our hearts and cleanse us of all unrighteousness. Remove all the barriers in us that prevent us from hearing from you clearly. Eliminate any hesitance about doing your perfect will and discovering your divine mandate for each one of us. Help us to be comfortable being different and living in a way that is contrary to the world around us. Tell us, Lord, what must we do in order to cross cultures and build bridges. Teach us how to engage cultures around us in a more compelling way. Show us, Lord, how to be real Christians, equipped to spread the good news about horizontal and vertical reconciliation. In Jesus' name, amen.

Reflection

What do you hear God saying in response to your prayer? Do you have a clearer understanding of your divine mandate? Are you prepared to take action that may be considered socially unpopular or different?

Application

Write down what you believe God is saying to you with regard to your divine mandate. Where is God sending you? What does God want you to do? Be as specific as possible. If necessary, spend more time in prayer in order to clearly discern the individual mandate for your life. If you are working through this with a group, discuss together what you are learning.

Accountability

Speak with another person in your group about your divine mandate. Check in regularly to see what steps each of you is taking to fulfill your mandate. Encourage each other by offering suggestions, assistance and prayer as needed.

CHAPTER 3: ENGAGE IN INTENTIONAL INTERACTION
Individual Reflection

1. How important is intentionality when you are an ambassador for Christ? Can you answer God's call to breaking down barriers if you don't do it on purpose?

2. Do you naturally gravitate toward people who are like you? What implications do you think that this has for your ability to be an effective evangelist?

3. How willing are you to be vulnerable and not totally in control in your efforts toward reconciliation? Are you willing to go to a place where you might not be fully conversant in the language or familiar with the customs?

Group Discussion and Application

1. Describe and discuss evangelism from an inductive and a deductive approach. How do they differ? Which is more consistent with an intentional and affirming effort toward reconciliation?

2. What will it take to get you to leave your comfort zone and go to where thirsty people are?

3. How can you be more intentional in your efforts to engage others who are not like you?

Prayer

God, give us a hunger to leave our comfort zone and go to unfamiliar places in order to spread your gospel. Help us to be comfortable being uncomfortable. We want to be intentional in our relationships and in reaching out to those who are not like us. Humble us to be good students and to ask thoughtful and sensitive questions when we are in different communities or cultures. Show us what we need to learn and give us the right heart to receive what we need to know in order to restore our credibility as Christians. Show us the "wells" that exist all around us and point us in the direction you would have us to go. In Jesus' name, amen.

Reflection

What group or people do you feel that you need to embrace? Where is the "well" where you can engage them? How do you feel about the prospect of going there?

Application

Once you have identified the cultural, racial, ethnic or gender group that you want to engage and the corresponding "well," plan an event or an activity that will take you there in a capacity to learn and share, not to give or help. You can create an exchange opportunity with members of your organization, ministry or church and members of a corresponding group in another community. You may want to initiate a dialogue around a current event that affects the group in an especially direct way.

Accountability

Assign a point person to lead this project and see it through. Once you have engaged in this process, revisit the "well." Continue to reach out to members of that community to be sure that the process is ongoing. Remember to remain intentional not only about the people you engage but also about the topics or issues involved in the events you plan.

CHAPTER 4: RELINQUISH POWER AND EMBRACE NEED
Individual Reflection

1. What is the motivation for your evangelism? Why do you want others to know Jesus?

Is your reason consistent or inconsistent with Jesus' model of evangelism?

Have you ever approached others from a pejorative notion of evangelism?

2. What do you genuinely need?

Can you envision something that a member of a different racial, ethnic, gender, socioeconomic or denominational background could provide to you that you really need? What is it?

3. Do you really *want* a diverse church, organization, school, etc., or do you feel that you "ought" to have one? Do you recognize the difference? Explain.

4. How comfortable are you being the "helped" instead of the "helper"? Why?

5. What kind of power do you have in your organization, institution or min-

istry? In what ways can you empower those of a different racial, ethnic, gender or cultural group?

Group Discussion and Application

1. Do you think most Christians approach non-Christians from a place of power? Why is this probably not be the most effective way to reach those who have been marginalized and culturally assaulted?

2. What does it contribute to the cause of reconciliation for people to feel needed, especially those who have not been valued by society? Why is interdependence important to advance the work of reconciliation?

3. In your organization, ministry or church, is it "nice" or "necessary" to have individuals from different racial, ethnic or cultural groups? What is the difference?

4. Has your organization, ministry or church ever unknowingly required that people relinquish their cultural or ethnic identity in order to be part of the group?

5. How could your organization, ministry or church be improved and enriched by the presence and contributions of individuals from different people groups? What effect might their presence have on your credibility as you spread the gospel?

Prayer

Lord, we thank you for the rich diversity you have woven into your kingdom. Teach us to appreciate the differences in each other and help us to understand and recognize the ways these differences help to make us all better. Help us not to be so arrogant as to believe that we don't need anything from anyone who is different from us. Unveil our eyes and show us what others have to offer that we really need. Help us to see how your image has been invested in every culture and people group. In Jesus' name, amen.

Reflection

Were you able to sense a real need in your organization, ministry or church? What is the need? How can you go about getting that need met in a way that affirms members of another cultural or ethnic or gender group, recognizing their unique and invaluable perspective?

Application

After identifying one genuine need of your organization, ministry or church, identify the human resources to meet that need, keeping in mind that the image of God is invested in all people groups and the best resource to meet the need may be someone who looks different from you. Assign a point person to invite a person or persons from this group to help your organization, ministry or church. Be sure to approach them from a place not of power but of affirmation and interdependence.

Accountability

Once the person or group has been identified and has accepted the invitation to join your organization, ministry or church, after a reasonable time has passed, the point person should check in with the new member(s) to see how they are doing and whether they are developing a sense of belonging. Make sure that they feel valued, affirmed and needed.

Chapter 5: Take Risks to Reach Out
Individual Reflection

1. Have you ever personally encountered a situation in which mistrust of the dominant culture was displayed? What effects did it have?

Do you understand why and how such mistrust can develop? What could you have done differently, if anything, to ameliorate the situation?

2. What might be some personal costs for you taking up the work of racial reconciliation? How might becoming an advocate for racial justice affect your friendships?

Group Discussion and Application

1. What risks do you take when you reach out to a person or group from a different racial, ethnic or cultural background?

2. What mistrust engendered by Christians might you encounter in addition to mistrust of you as a member of a different cultural or social group?

Prayer

Lord, we ask you to give us the strength to continue in the struggle for racial justice despite the costs. Help us to see the costs but still to persevere, knowing that building your kingdom on earth as it is in heaven is worth the price. We pray that you would use us as instruments to rebuild trust. Help us to reflect an integrity that is worthy of you. Shield our hearts from taking any rejection, anger or hostility personally, and cover us with your peace. In Jesus' name, amen.

Reflection
Were any costs or risks revealed to you that you didn't expect or identify previously? Have those costs and risks affected your commitment to seeking the restoration of the gospel's credibility?

Application
In light of your chosen activity and action from chapters one and three, outline the potential risks and costs associated with implementing the various activities you have chosen. Devise a plan to help minimize these costs.

Accountability
Revise your plans of action begun in chapters one and three in light of the costs and risks discovered in this chapter. Adjust timelines as necessary but continue with the projects as planned.

CHAPTER 6: DEVELOP RECIPROCITY AND INTERDEPENDENCE
Individual Reflection
1. What things of value do you have to offer in an evangelistic relationship?
2. How can you encourage and affirm the value of everyone in your ministry?
3. Why do you think it is important for the American church to recognize its interdependence with the global church?

Group Discussion and Application
1. In what ways can you help those in your organization or church use their gifts to foster mutual relationships?
2. Do you think that assimilation is helpful to restoring our Christian credibility? Why or why not?

3. Why is it important for people to know themselves, to be who they are and to know that they have something unique to offer?

4. What does reciprocity look like in relationships?

How does this reflect real Christianity?

Prayer

God, help us to fully see ourselves as we are and to fully see the problems that exist in this world, but help us not to get stuck in head shaking and hand wringing. Enable us to take wise action instead. Help us to build relationships of mutuality and reciprocity, where all parties understand that they have something of value to offer. We don't want to obliterate any group or culture's identity; instead we want to celebrate the particular gifts that you have so generously given to each of us. In Jesus' name, amen.

Reflection

What did you hear God saying in your prayer? Did you sense any direction to take in building relationships of mutuality and reciprocity?

Application

In the application section for chapter three you were asked to invite members of another cultural, racial or ethnic group to join your organization because they had something of vital importance to you. Examine your relationship with that individual or group. Is it characterized by mutuality and reciprocity? If not, take steps to make it so; if it is, take steps to improve it further.

Accountability

Begin a thoughtful dialogue with the individual(s) who have recently joined your organization regarding their perspective on the relationship. If needed, seek their help in making the relationship a more mutual one. Ask for ways they can reciprocate.

CHAPTER 7: GO BEYOND THE SUPERFICIAL
Individual Reflection

1. What are some of your unspoken needs? In what ways have you gone about trying to get them met?

2. In what ways has the insatiable nature of sin been an impediment to your faith walk and relationship with Jesus?

Why is it important to recognize it not only for ourselves but in our witness to others?

Group Discussion and Application

1. How can your organization, ministry or church present Jesus in a more intriguing way that causes people to want to know more?

What does doing so require of you?

2. How important is it to move beyond superficial conversation when having evangelistic encounters with others?

3. What are the different types of external resources you have used to quench your thirst? How have those efforts proven to be temporary when compared to the eternal resource Jesus offers us?

4. Why do you think that people are reluctant to identify and surrender the counterfeit thirst-quencher when Jesus offers the "real thing"?

Prayer

Lord, help us to identify the counterfeits we have used to try and quench our thirst and the external things we use to define ourselves. Give us the courage to move beyond the temporary comfort these actions, behaviors, people and things provide, and endue us with the power and the will to surrender these external resources to you so that we can make room for the internal resource of your Spirit. Show us how to present Jesus in an intriguing way so that people will want to know more about him and will want to receive the living water that only he can supply. In Jesus's name, amen.

Reflection

Did you sense a revelation of any counterfeits or external resources that you had not previously identified? How do you feel about the possibility of giving those things, behaviors, actions or people up?

Application

Honestly identify the external resources that you have used to define yourself.

Create a collective opportunity to give those things to Jesus. For example, you could plan a service including the Scripture reading from John 4 and appropriate worship songs, and ask each person to bring a representatin of the "counterfeit" and provide an opportunity to give them to Jesus.

Accountability

Now that you have identified your counterfeits and surrendered them to Jesus, get support from an individual or organization particular to your area of need. Join a community of like-minded people who can encourage you. Spend time with God, in prayer, reading the Bible or quietly seeking his presence to strengthen you on your journey.

CHAPTER 8: BE AUTHENTIC AND TRANSPARENT IN WORSHIP

Individual Reflection

1. In the course of your spiritual journey, have you ever *pretended* to be a Christian? When?

2. What "wells" have you sought to quench your emotional and spiritual thirsts? What would Jesus tell you to go back and get, as he told Sam to go and get her husband?

3. What does spiritual authenticity mean to you?

4. How can worship be a unifying experience?

Group Discussion and Application

1. How has the lack of spiritual authenticity in the church led to a lack of credibility for the church?

2. Read Revelation 7:9. How does your church, institution, organization or ministry reflect the vision described in this Scripture passage?

3. Why is the transforming power of worship essential in the process to be spiritually authentic?

4. Why is spiritual authenticity crucial in evangelistic efforts?

Prayer

God, teach us how to worship you in spirit and in truth. Reveal to us how and when we come to you in a less than honest way, pretending to be someone we are not. Open our hearts to receive the fullness of Jesus' sacrifice on the cross, by which you receive us as we really are. We pray against any fear of rejection, which may have prevented us from worshiping you authentically in the past. Help us to be less concerned with the form of our worship than with the truth of our worship. In Jesus' name, amen.

Reflection

Do you feel God calling you from the shadows of your shame, insecurities and pretending? Who does God say that you really are?

Application

Create an atmosphere within your group or team for an authentic worship experience. Draw on the resources and the relationships you have developed in the application sections of chapters 1-7 and use worship music, visual symbols and prayer to facilitate a racially, culturally and ethnically diverse experience. Be sure to honor the different church denominations and traditions that may be represented.

Accountability

After the worship experience, discuss your individual experiences. Did you feel that you could be authentic? Did you feel uncomfortable? At peace? Embraced?

CHAPTER 9: MAKE A LIFE-CHANGING DECISION
Individual Reflection

1. At what point in your life did you make a life-changing decision to enter into a relationship with Jesus?

2. What did you have to exchange for the "living water" that only Jesus can provide?

3. What is your story? How have you let Jesus rewrite your story? How do you think your story can be effective in leading others to Christ?

4. Do you need another conversion to the whole truth of the gospel story—one that gives equal emphasis to the vertical and horizontal dimensions of reconciliation through the cross?

Group Discussion and Application

1. How is a relationship with Jesus different from religious Christianity? How has the "religion" of Christianity caused damage to the credibility of Christians?

2. Why is it a leap of faith to move beyond the limits of our ethnocentrism and envision a kingdom community?

3. How does Jesus bring people's stories in line with his story to give them a new storyline? What is the new storyline?

Prayer

Heavenly Father, we appreciate the example of the Samaritan woman, and like her, we receive Jesus as the One who can make sense of our lives, the One who can answer every question and calm every fear. Help us to surrender our lack in exchange for your sufficiency and our inadequacy for your completeness. Reveal to us how our counterfeit methods of trying to satisfy our thirst have left us thirsty, and give us instead a thirst for your living waters. Help us to make the most important decision of our lives, to enter into an authentic relationship with you and to share the whole truth of your gospel message--that you came to reconcile us to you and to each other. In Jesus' name, amen.

Reflection

Are there things that you have been unwilling to exchange with Jesus? What are they? Why has it been hard to let go of these things? How has your reluctance hindered you in advancing your relationship with Christ?

Application

Write down your story. Notice where Jesus enters your story and how he changes the narrative. Does your story say what you thought it did? Why or why not? Is there a further conversion that you need to experience?

Accountability

Chose another person in your group and share stories. Discuss ways in which your story could help you to close the credibility gap and bring others to Christ.

CHAPTER 10: TAKE ACTION TO BE COUNTERCULTURAL
Individual Reflection

1. What are some of the "unspoken rules" that you might have to break to promote racial reconciliation in your organization, church or community?

2. In what ways can you stand up for racial justice in your organization, church or community?

3. In what ways does the gospel influence the way you vote? Do you agree that it should?

Group Discussion and Application

1. What would it look like to be "countercultural" in your church, organization, or ministry? What might you have to do? Give some concrete examples.

2. Reread the excerpt from Martin Luther King's "Letter from Birmingham Jail." Do you agree with his contention that creating tension is a necessary part of the work of racial reconciliation? Why or why not? Does that make you feel uncomfortable?

3. Do you believe that most Christians have practiced what they preach in terms of unity, peace and reconciliation? How do you feel that this has affected our credibility?

Prayer

Lord, we ask you to give us the courage to put feet to our faith in order to be credible witnesses for you. Show us constructive ways to be countercultural in our church, organization or community. Create a tension inside each of us for racial justice and reconciliation. Give us discernment to understand when we should take action, and what action to take. Develop humility in us so that we establish appropriate credibility with those to whom we want to be a bridge. Surround us with those who will support and understand us, but give us a strong sense of your presence when we have to stand alone. In Jesus' name, amen.

Reflection

In what area do you feel a constructive tension? Do you feel any leading to address this tension?

Application

Chose one concrete example of countercultural social action discovered in response to group discussion question 1 and implement it in your organization, church or ministry.

Accountability

What is your anticipated response to your countercultural social action?

Once you have implemented the action chosen, reflect upon your anticipated response and compare with the actual response. How was it different?

CHAPTER 11: BE A BRIDGE BUILDER
Individual Reflection

1. With which communities do you have influence?

2. How can you build bridges to these communities for people from a different racial, ethnic or cultural group?

3. As a leader in your organization or church, you can likely identify some people who will listen to you but might not listen to others. How can you use your influence to encourage reconciliation within the organization?

Group Discussion and Application

1. What does it mean to be a bridge builder?

Why are bridge builders necessary in order to close the credibility gap?

2. How are bridge builders connected to our need to be spiritually authentic in order to establish credibility within our community and in communities of different racial and ethnic backgrounds?

Prayer

Lord, help us to live a life beyond reproach, so that others will have no problem attesting to our authenticity and integrity as representatives of your kingdom. Teach us how to build bridges in the communities where we are insiders and have history. Open our eyes to show us areas where we have influence. Reveal opportunities to build bridges and create unlikely partnerships and relationships for your glory. In Jesus' name, amen.

Reflection

What do you hear God saying to your heart as a result of this prayer? Does any particular opportunity to build a bridge resonate in your spirit?

Application

As a group, watch the movie *Do the Right Thing,* which is discussed in this chapter. As you are watching, notice the bridge builders and how they do (or do not) use their influence to help the various cultures in this Brooklyn neighborhood get along. Discuss what each could have done differently, if anything, to avoid the eventual conflict between the groups. How effective do you think the bridge builders were? What leads you to this conclusion?

Accountability

Taking all that you have learned about the credibility gap that exists between Christians and non-Christians (and even within the Christian community), determine how you will be a bridge builder. Share your plan with the group and discuss steps to take in building the bridge. Come back at an agreed-upon time to share your experiences.

CONCLUSION: TAKING THE WITNESS STAND
Individual Reflection

1. What is the second conversion discussed in this chapter? Do you agree or disagree with its premise? Why or why not?

2. What role does the Holy Spirit play in global evangelization across racial, cultural and ethnic lines?

Group Discussion and Application

1. Read Ephesians 2. Discuss how this passage calls us to an inclusive kingdom community that embraces all cultures and racial and ethnic groups.

2. How is justice integral to discipleship?

3. How are evangelism and conversion treated as reconciliation in 2 Corinthians 5? What are the implications for our interpersonal relationships?

4. Refer to the diagram on page 131. Identify your Jerusalem, Judea and Samaria. What is necessary for you to go through each setting in order to reach the

world? What environments can you expect to encounter in each?

Prayer

God, give us the desire and the tools to reclaim the credibility of the church. Show us how we can invite people into discipleship—a holistic, transformative relationship with the Lord Jesus Christ. Stir in us a passion for justice; use us to create right relationships, relationships in which wounds and hurts are acknowledged and healed, sins are forgiven and wrongs are set right. We need your power and strength to practice and preach this message. We want a new humanity to be created. We are dependent and reliant on you. In Jesus' name, amen.

Reflection

What has God stirred in you as a result of this prayer? How is he leading you to invite others to discipleship?

Application

Discuss and write down the core changes that have come about in you and in your organization or church because you have initiated the work of closing the credibility gap. Do you feel that you have been successful? Have any perceptions about you or your organization or church changed? Do you feel more or less credible as a witness for Jesus Christ?

Accountability

Establish a committee or task force to take up the issues addressed by the book on an ongoing basis. Plan to meet regularly to evaluate progress. Encourage the participation of members of various racial, ethnic and cultural groups. Plan new events, outreaches, "well" visits and discussions to continue to remain credible.

FURTHER READING

Ahn, Che'. *Fire Evangelism*. Grand Rapids: Chosen Books, 2006.

Barna, George. *The Second Coming of the Church*. Nashville: Word Publishers, 1998.

Brown, Raymond E. *The Gospel According to John*. Anchor Bible Commentary. New York: Doubleday, 1966.

Campolo, Tony, and Mary Albert Darling. *The God of Intimacy and Action: Reconnecting Ancient Spiritual Practices, Evangelism, and Justice*. San Francisco: Jossey-Bass, 2007.

Hybels, Bill. *Just Walk Across the Room: Simple Steps to Pointing People to Faith*. Grand Rapids: Zondervan, 2006.

The Essential IVP Reference Collection. Downers Grove, Ill.: InterVarsity Press, 2001.

McKenzie, Vashti M. *Journey to the Well: Twelve Lessons on Personal Transformation*. New York: Viking Compass, 2002.

Moore, York. *Growing Your Faith and Giving It Away*. Downers Grove, Ill.: InterVarsity Press, 2005.

Peterson, Eugene H. *The Message: The Bible in Contemporary Language*. Colorado Springs: NavPress, 2002.

Priest, Robert J., and Alvaro L. Nieves. *This Side of Heaven: Race, Ethnicity and Christian Faith*. New York: Oxford University Press, 2007.

Raybon, Patricia. *I Told the Mountain to Move: Learning to Pray so Things Change*. Wheaton, Ill.: SaltRiver, 2005.

Richardson, Richard. *Evangelism Outside the Box*. Downers Grove, Ill.: InterVarsity Press, 2000.

Richardson, Richard. *Reimagining Evangelism*. Downers Grove, Ill.: InterVarsity Press, 2006.

Winner, Lauren F. *Girl Meets God*. New York: Random House, 2002.

NOTES

Introduction: Becoming a Credible Witness

p. 18   A *Chicago Tribune* article: Ron Grossman, "A Camp They Can Believe In," *Chicago Tribune*, June 27, 2007, available at http:www.chicagotribune.com/news/nationworld/chi-campatheist_27june27,1,452407.story?ctrack=3& cset=true.

pp. 18-19   Christian demographer George Barna: Simon McIntyre, review of *Evangelism that Works* by George Barna (Regal Books), Christian City Church International, 1997.

p. 19   The U.S. Census Bureau predicts: CNNfyi.com, "Population Growth Will Foster Demographic Shift," available at http://archives.cnn.com/2000/fyi/teacher.resources/lesson.plans/03/23/population.

p. 19   "Census data from March 2002": Leila Gonzalez Sullivan, "Do We Need Targeted Leadership Development Programs?" National Community College Hispanic Council (NCCHC) Leadership Fellows Program, available at http://ced.ncsu.edu/ahe/ncchc/resources/monograph.pdf, accessed July 11, 2007.

p. 19   Meanwhile the Asian: CNNfyi.com, "Population Growth Will Foster Demographic Shift."

p. 19   A study conducted by veteran demographer: "The Blending of the United States," available at http://usinfo.state.gov/journals/itsv/0699/ijse/stanfld.htm.

p. 22   "Muslim publics": http://pewglobal.org/reports/display.php?ReportID=247, accessed July 10, 2007.

p. 22   "The world's fastest": William Poole (president, Federal Reserve Bank of St. Louis), "World Population Trends and Challenges," address given at Lincoln University, Jefferson City, Missouri, October 4, 2004, available at http://stlouisfed.org/news/speeches/2004.

p. 22   "has an advantage": http://education.stateuniversity.com/pages/2556/Youth-Demographic-Trends.html.

p. 23   Younger Americans seem: George Barna, *The Second Coming of the Church* (Nashville: Word, 1998), p. 55.

p. 23   "Despite all the differences": Bruce Ellis Benson, "What Is Postmodernism?" September 14, 2005, available at http://www.anewkindofconversation.com.

Chapter 1: Know My Context to Know My Story

p. 28   "Jesus realized that": Eugene H. Peterson, *The Message: The Bible in Contemporary Language* (Colorado Springs: NavPress, 2002), pp. 1922-24.

p. 30   "The Samaritans are": Raymond E. Brown, *The Gospel According to John*, Anchor Bible Commentary 29-29A (New York: Doubleday, 1966-1977), p. 170.

p. 30   The Samaritans emerged: Tite Tiénou, "The Samaritans: A Biblical-Theological Mirror for Understanding Racial, Ethnic and Religious Identity?" in *This Side of Heaven: Race, Ethnicity and Christian Faith*, ed. Robert J. Priest and Alvaro L. Nieves (New York: Oxford University Press, 2007), p. 216.

p. 31   "psychologists and historians": Claudia Wallis, "Why Did They Do It?" *Time*, May 9, 2004, available at http://www.time.com/time/printout/0,8816,634639,00.html.

pp. 32-33   "The Samaritans received: Commentary on Matthew 10:5 in Barnes' Notes (electronic database), Biblesoft, 1997.

p. 33   "Samaria became a place": Ibid.

p. 34   "A Jewish regulation": Brown, *Gospel According to John*, p. 170.

p. 34   "perpetual menstruate": C. K. Barrett cites from Nidah 4.1 that "the daughters of the Samaritans are menstruants from their childhood," implying that they are all the time unclean women. For discussion on untouchability and impurity associated with the Samaritans, see C. K. Barrett, *The Gospel According to St. John: An Introduction with Commentary and Notes on the Greek Text* (Philadelphia: Westminster Press, 1978), p. 32.

Chapter 2: Begin with a Divine Mandate

p. 41   "The enduring social": Alan Berube and Elizabeth Kneebone, "Two Steps Back: City and Suburban Poverty Trends, 1999-2005," Brookings Institution, Living Cities Census Series, December 2006, p. 1.

p. 42   "The Jews, after their return": Commentary on Matthew 10:5 in Barnes' Notes.

Chapter 3: Engage in Intentional Interaction

p. 51   Samaria was "situated": Commentary on Matthew 10:5 in Barnes' Notes (electronic database), Biblesoft, 1997.

p. 51   The well Jesus sat by: Ibid.

Chapter 4: Relinquish Power and Embrace Need

p. 60   This beautiful city was "built": Commentary on Isaiah 28:1 in Barnes Notes (electronic database), Biblesoft, 1997.

p. 65   According to *Webster's Dictionary*: *Webster's New World Dictionary*, 3rd college ed. (New York: Simon and Schuster, 1988), p. 1058.

p. 65   "power is the ability": Martin Luther King Jr., in Taylor Branch, "I Have Seen the Promised Land," *Time*, January 1, 2006, available at http://www.time.com/time/printout/0,8816,1145260,00.html.

p. 66   If a woman could not cook: R. H. Stein, "Divorce," in *Dictionary of Jesus and the Gospels,* ed. Joel B. Green, Scot McKnight and I. Howard Marshall (Downers Grove, Ill.: InterVarsity Press, 1992), p. 196.

p. 68   "hybrid culture": Curtiss DeYoung, Michael Emerson, George Yancy and Karen Chai Kim, *United by Faith: The Multicultural Congregation as an Answer to the Problem of Race* (London: Oxford University Press, 2003), p. 168.

pp. 68-69   "This hybrid culture has the effect": Brian Howell, "Power and Reconciliation in an Urban Church," in *This Side of Heaven: Race, Ethnicity and Christian Faith,* ed. Robert J. Priest and Alvaro L. Nieves (New York: Oxford University Press, 2007), p. 297.

Chapter 6: Develop Reciprocity and Interdependence

p. 89   "A gospel that merely": Rick Richardson, *Evangelism Outside the Box* (Downers Grove, Ill.: InterVarsity Press, 2000), p. 126.

p. 90   "We are all caught": Martin Luther King Jr., "Letter from a Birmingham Jail," April 16, 1963, available online at www.stanford.edu/group/King/popular_requests/frequentdocs/birmingham.pdf.

Chapter 8: Be Authentic and Transparent in Worship

p. 101   This fueled an irreconcilable: Commentary on Matthew 10:5 in Barnes' Notes (electronic database), Biblesoft, 1997; and Adam Clarke's Commentary (electronic database), Biblesoft, 1996.

pp. 102-3   "Human beings were made": Rick Richardson, *Evangelism Outside the Box* (Downers Grove, Ill.: InterVarsity Press, 2000), p. 126.

p. 104   In Richardson's words: Ibid., p. 46.

Chapter 9: Make a Life-Changing Decision

p. 111   "We can't even imagine": Sarah E. Hinlicky, "Talking to Generation X," *Critique* 7 (1999): 4 (available from Ransom Fellowship, 1150 W. Center Street, Rochester, MN 55902).

Chapter 10: Take Action to Be Countercultural

pp. 118-19   "You may well ask": Martin Luther King Jr., "Letter from a Birmingham Jail," April 16, 1963, available online at www.standford.edu/group/King/popular_requests/frequentdocs/birmingham.pdf.

p. 119   "Most Asian Americans should recognize": "Asian American Leaders Criticize AsianWeek for Printing Kenneth Eng's Column 'Why I Hate Blacks,' " asianweek.com, February 23, 2007.

Chapter 11: Be a Bridge Builder

p. 124   "I believe that ten": Bill Hybels, *Just Walk Across the Room: Simple Steps Pointing People to Faith* (Grand Rapids: Zondervan, 2006), p. 165.

p. 126   "Living water exists": Ibid., p. 166.

Conclusion: Taking the Witness Stand

p. 131   It is a faith that transcends: Eric John Wyckoff, "Jesus in Samaria (John 4:4-12): A Model for Cross-Cultural Ministry," *Biblical Theology Bulletin,* September 22, 2005. Available online at http://www.encyclopedia.com/doc/1G1-137016447.htm.

salter mcneil & associates, llc

igniting a passion for reconciliation

Dr. Brenda Salter McNeil is the founder and president of Salter McNeil & Associates, LLC. This company facilitates an intercultural competency process in partnership with Christian leaders to transform organizations. To learn more about this reconciliation ministry and their speaking, training and consulting services, please contact Salter McNeil & Associates at:

7115 W. North Avenue #293, Oak Park, IL. 60302

773.583.8085   www.saltermcneil.com   (fax) 773.290.8247